Steam in the Sussex Landscape

The scene just north of Hamsey Crossing on 7th July 1951, as H2 Class Atlantic locomotive No. 32425 *Trevose Head* attacks the stiff climb towards Cooksbridge with the 5.48 p.m. relief boat train from Newhaven Harbour to Victoria. The locomotive has its work cut out on the 1 in 143 gradient hauling a substantial load of eleven carriages, including a buffet car, plus a couple of vans. The railway at this point is running parallel with the River Ouse, which is half a mile away. Beyond the river ran the Lewes to Uckfield line, closed in the late 1960s, both routes taking advantage of the gap in the downs at this location.

J.J. Smith

H2 Class Atlantic No. 32422 *North Foreland* creates a powerful image as it makes an energetic exit from Newhaven with the 5.58 p.m. boat train to Victoria on 12th August 1951.

J.J. Smith

Steam in the Sussex Landscape

Klaus Marx

Michael S. Welch

Beautifully lit by the low winter sunshine, B2X Class No. 317 enters Ford Station with a Brighton to Portsmouth train on 2nd February 1914. On the left the signalman poses at the window of his old style 'Brighton' signal box, while the Arun bridge is just visible in the distance. The interesting three-way points provided access to a siding which descended to a wharf by the river. The small white-painted building adjacent to the siding was used as a blacksmith's shop. The road to Arundel, in the foreground, was built and maintained by the railway company, which charged users a toll until responsibility was transferred to the West Sussex County Council in 1938.   *Lens of Sutton*

Runpast Publishing, 10 Kingscote Grove, Cheltenham GL51 6JX
Typeset by Ryburn Typesetting Ltd, Luddendenfoot, Halifax
Printed by The Amadeus Press Ltd, Huddersfield
© Klaus Marx, Michael S. Welch, Runpast Publishing, 1990
ISBN 1 870754 16 6

INTRODUCTION

The railways of Sussex have been a popular subject with publishers in recent years, but this album is believed to be the first solely devoted to steam traction in the county. What is more, we have adopted a new approach by relating the railway routes to the countryside which they traverse. The downs, rivers, woodlands and coastline of Sussex feature strongly in many of the pictures, so this album is as much a book of Sussex country scenes as a collection of railway photographs. In some cases we have selected pictures which fall outside the strict interpretation of the word 'landscape', but feel that certain illustrations were worthy of inclusion due to their particular historical merit. The charming picture of Littlehampton engine shed in 1938, and the very rare shot of the last-remaining E1R Class locomotive at Eastbourne depot while *en route* to Ashford Works for breaking-up come into this category.

In the search for material more than fifty photographers in various parts of the country have been contacted, and at times it has been difficult trying to locate suitable material of the required pictorial type. In steam days many photographers contented themselves with either 'station platform' views or portraits of locomotives reposing on shed, which were not suitable for our purposes. Perhaps the most remarkable fact about Sussex railways portrayed by the pictures is the amazing variety of locomotive types seen in the county even as late as 1960. Most of these are illustrated, together with a selection of 'foreign' motive power from other regions. We were delighted to trace photographs of such unaccustomed classes as an LM&SR 'Jubilee' 4-6-0, L&NER B1 Class 4-6-0 and even a rare shot of an *ex*-War Department 2-8-0, some of which worked in Sussex for a brief period following the second world war.

We would like to record our gratitude to the many photographers who kindly provided material for this album. Without their help the project would never have come to fruition, and we are deeply grateful to them all. A special mention of the outstanding contribution to this volume made by John J. Smith is appropriate. He was a prolific photographer of the Sussex steam scene, and produced beautifully artistic pictures many of which grace the pages of this album. Readers may be interested to know that the picture research for this album was the responsibility of Michael S. Welch, while Klaus Marx wrote the captions.

K.M.
M.S.W.
August 1990

BR Standard 2-6-4T locomotive No. 80013 takes the Eridge line at Groombridge Junction with a Brighton-bound train on 14th May 1960. These well-proportioned machines were a regular sight on most East Sussex branch lines during the final years of steam, and were one of the last active classes in the area.

D.W. Winkworth

THE SUSSEX LANDSCAPE

General Description

The term *Weald* is regarded as comprising the North and South Downs and the intermediary areas of sands and clays of the Cretaceous Period. Though extending into the adjoining counties, the largest section and central core lies within the county boundaries of East and West Sussex. It is a young region in the great time perspective of Britain's geological history, being once submerged by the sea when the various sands, chalk and clays were deposited, the central Weald later surviving as a large salt water bay.

These strata in later millennia folded up into a great dome which, like the removal of the top of an egg, was eroded away to reveal the oldest rocks in the middle and the youngest at the edges. There was not just one fold but several, causing variations in the basic rock sequence, nevertheless the broad features of the geology of the area are easily readable from its landscape. The horseshoe of chalk, the limbs of which are formed by the South and North Downs, contains a semi-circle of clay and central block of sand or sandstone.

The South Downs

The most prominent feature of the Sussex landscape, visible from far north in the county, is the downland chalk stretching from north of Chichester as far as Beachy Head. The prevalent chalk is a remarkably pure limestone, nearly 95% calcium carbonate, that creates that glistening white backcloth to so many Sussex photographs. Where it meets the coast it produces the most dramatic cliff scenery, notably in Newhaven and Seaford. Nevertheless, the cliffs are retreating as they have done ever since the sea's first incursion made Britain an island some 8,000 years ago. Where it was punctuated by deep coombs and river valleys such as the Arun, Adur and Cuckmere, the railway followed. Coombs are deep basin-shaped hollows fictitiously associated with the devil 'who seems to have all the best landscapes as well as the best tunes' – hence the Devil's Dyke legend. Where directness of route to the coast was the primary consideration, tunnelling was necessary, hence three occurred in the vicinity of Singleton and Cocking, another south of Amberley through a projection of chalk, and at Clayton, Patcham, Holland Road, Kemp Town, Falmer and Lewes. The route of the former Dyke branch represents a remarkable stiff climb up the downland grades to the breathtaking escarpment overlooking Poynings.

The Downs are built of three layers of chalk – the marly Lower Chalk forms a low platform below the Downs, the Middle the steep faces of the escarpments, whilst the Upper covers the plateau, and between the three chalk series lie harder layers known as Melbourne Rock, a source of building stone, notably quarried near Cocking. Scars of old and new workings like those at Amberley, Beeding, Rodmell and Southerham, abound in the Downs, especially where close to waterways. Also found in the chalk are flints, a form of silica derived from bodies of creatures that inhabited the chalk seas.

The Greensands

On the inland scarp of the South Downs lies the greensand belt consisting of the Upper Greensand, Gault and Lower Greensand, fairly similar in width except around Midhurst where the latter extends for several miles. The name 'Greensand' was due to coloration by algae when the central Weald was a salt-water lake. This rock produces some of the most delightful landscapes in the region, together with some of the most attractive building stone and fine sand which is quarried.

Between the two greensands, like a wet sandwich, is the gault clay, so sticky and unstable that it is known locally as 'blue slipper'. It began as mud deposited on the ancient sea floor, was easily eroded by running water and caused much anguish to railway engineers – classic examples at the other end of the horseshoe of gault in Kent were the dramatic landslips in Folkestone Warren. The gault clay is an important source of red brick and tile manufacture and it was used extensively by Joseph Firbank on the Midhurst, Bluebell and Cuckoo lines. Cocking, Elsted, Rogate and Wivelsfield were centres of the industry.

The Wealden Clay

The outcrop of overlying Wealden Clay shapes up on the map facing east like the open jaws of an alligator. It forms a wide strike vale, mainly of very gentle relief, though with variations in the thickness of the beds. Particularly in the west, thin seams of sandstone and limestone give rise to slight features. The latter, known as Sussex Marble or Winkle Clay, was formed by freshwater snails trapped by silting in the Wealden lake, notably around Petworth. Impressive in the extreme west, it soon diminishes in height, cut into by the transverse valley of the Arun, and thins out rapidly in East Sussex.

On this belt were to be found numerous brickworks, at Midhurst, Warnham, Horsham, Southwater, Burgess Hill and Berwick. Most of the branches west of the Brighton main line traversed the undulating Wealden Clay – studded with coppices – as did the lower sections of the Bluebell and Cuckoo lines, both sections of lines that branched at Keymer Junction for Brighton and Lewes, the line between Southwater and Henfield, and that from Three Bridges to Horsham and down towards Amberley.

The Central Weald

This is the heart and core of the region containing some of the most spectacular land forms. The central Wealden heights with their gently rounded ridges, seamed by deeply cut ghylls which widen out and join together to form broad river valleys mainly heading east and west, reflect in their minor relief features and in changes of vegetation the various basic cretacious rocks. These Wealden strata are separable into five major divisions, two of sandstone and three of clay, but chequered throughout the whole area like a patchwork quilt, frequently faulted and varying in resistance to erosion.

The largest patches on the surface are of Tunbridge Wells Sand, locally known as Grinstead Clay and Cuckfield Clay in parts of West Sussex where it stretches as far as Horsham. Other railway points laid on this surface include Eridge, West Hoathly, Uckfield and Hellingly. Pevensey stands on another small outcrop.

Another expansive group is comprised of Ashdown Sand, serving the railways which crossed Ashdown Forest at such points as East Grinstead, Hartfield, Horsted Keynes, and Heathfield, with a broad strip running from Uckfield eastwards to Winchelsea. Formations of Wadhurst Clay appear over most of the central Weald – near East

The classic panorama looking towards the River Ouse from Southerham Junction was a favourite amongst Sussex railway photographers, and looking at this superb view, taken in September 1953, it is easy to understand why. The train, hauled by K Class Mogul No. 32340, is the 7.35 a.m. from Birkenhead Woodside to Hastings formed of a Bulleid 3-set, of the batch built by BRCW Co., supplemented by a Maunsell side-corridor vehicle. The picture is full of interest, and remarkably includes a sailing barge berthed at a riverside wharf serving Eastwoods cement works. The little tunnel under the railway accommodates a footpath which has left the towpath along the river to connect with the main coast road. The photograph is further enhanced by a magnificent trail of black smoke from the locomotive's chimney, and the superb cloud formation. *J.J. Smith*

Grinstead, Horsted Keynes, Cuckfield, Uckfield, Hailsham, Crowhurst, Wadhurst, Hastings and Rye. It provided the bulk of locations for the iron ore smelted in the renowned Wealden ironworks of East Sussex.

Fairlight Clay formed the lowest of the various strata known collectively as the Hastings Beds, varying from soft clay to tough sandstone. Small outcrops appeared all over the Weald, predominantly around Bexhill and Hastings, between which the railway had to be tunnelled through the tough sandstone and again out towards Ore. This rock also appears at East Grinstead, Haywards Heath, Three Bridges and Horsham. An example of the vast variations in weathering can be seen near West Hoathly and Kingscote, where the valley of Rocks Wood has been cut through the sandstone to the underlying Wadhurst Clay leaving a striking wall of rock each side of the valley. This wall has been separated into units by weathering processes leaving outcrops of high standing rock, one of which has been named 'Great upon Little'. Similar examples exist at Imberhorne and right on the county border at High Rocks.

The final material to complete the Wealden quilt is a small inlay of Purbeck Beds near Mountfield, initiating the long history of gypsum traffic there.

The Rivers

The rivers, which rise in the heart of the Weald and produce some of the loveliest Sussex scenery, at first sight conform to the symmetry of the geological structure, flowing north and south to the

Thames and to the Channel, respectively. But the pattern is not a simple one and has been likened more to a trellis, for the rivers seek the weaker rock outcrops and exploit them, taking the easiest course.

Both the Mole and the Ouse rise in Worth Forest; the latter involves a masterly viaduct near Balcombe and is closely followed for three miles by the line from Sheffield Park to Barcombe, and from Lewes south to Newhaven, where the coming of the railway and the upgrading of the harbour in 1847 necessitated changing the course of the Ouse, straightening the river mouth and constructing a breakwater to the detriment of the medieval port of Seaford. The line through Ashurst and Cowden passes over several tributaries of the Medway, which rises near Kingscote, and the hilly environs of East Grinstead are divided by incisions of a number of infant rivers, involving the railway coming in from the south across an impressive viaduct at Imberhorne.

The Wey/Arun watershed is the high ridge of greensand marked by Baynards Tunnel, also the county boundary on the Guildford–Horsham line. The Mole/Arun watershed is at Faygate. South of Pulborough the Mid-Sussex line follows the Arun to the coast. The Adur has its main source near Billingshurst, the lesser one rises south of Haywards Heath, and its valley is followed for most of its length by the Steyning line which crosses the river three times on its way to Shoreham. The station area of Brighton, incidentally, sits snugly in the valley of a former downland stream, now largely lost to view, which involved the London Road and Lewes Road viaducts as well as the building of the station, sheds, works and trackwork supported along the shelf of the valley to Preston Park.

The Kentish Rother has its source at Rotherfield but flows predominantly eastwards to the Walland marshes and Rye, since the Crowborough Beacons form a watershed between it and the Ouse. The Sussex Rother rises in Hampshire and, instead of using the East Dean valley down to Chichester, flows east past Midhurst to its junction with the Arun at Pulborough, where Hardham Junction lies in the flood plain of the Arun/Rother confluence.

The Coastal Reaches

While the chalk cliffs and headlands along the coast from Hastings to Brighton continue to be eroded, the land lost has been compensated for by new areas in recent centuries. To the east of Hastings lie the marshes of Romney and Walland, fed by the rivers Brede, Tillingham and Rother and screened by the ever-increasing barrier of shingle thrown up around Dungeness. Between Bexhill and Eastbourne lie the Pevensey levels, similarly screened by the shingle stretching eastwards from the Crumbles. Such areas, once below sea level, were filled up at the estuaries by the material the rivers were carrying. To this can be added land reclamation by means of sea defences, groynes and breakwaters which have stemmed erosion and caused the silting up of marshes. The dunes at West Wittering and the sands at Camber now lie well inland as do the former ports of Rye and Winchelsea. Westwards from Worthing runs the ever widening Sussex Plain, encompassing Bognor and Chichester and the creeks of Bosham and Selsey. In terms of railway construction the coastal plain presented few problems involving civil engineering, though the fact that so many roads were crossed on the level west of Brighton has been a cause for regret in more recent times. The Sussex Plain contained within it a wealth of flints and gravels, particularly at Lavant, and also had left on it by the receding ice massive boulders of granite and basalt such as can be seen at West Worthing, Hotham Park at Bognor and Stanmer Park at Brighton.

River estuaries were always an awkward problem, as river traffic vied with rail, but the difficulty was overcome in a variety of different ways. The coast line went across the Adur estuary by means of a trestle bridge, replaced in 1892, whilst both the Arun at Ford and the Ouse at Southerham had movable bridges to carry over the line, for shipping was, until quite recent times, still going up as far as Arundel and Lewes, respectively. The West Side Tramway at Newhaven also crossed the Ouse on a swing bridge. But views of the sea from the railway carriage are few and far between, Rye and Winchelsea being well inland these days, Bexhill to Pevensey being largely screened by heaped-up shingle and lines of beach huts, while the West Coast line was routed some miles inland with views seaward being blocked by housing developments. Even the Selsey Tramway was cut back from Selsey Beach to the Town station prior to the first world war. Glimpses can, however, be obtained between Newhaven and Seaford, and at the crossings of the river estuaries previously mentioned. For fortunate engine crews of shunters at Newhaven, Shoreham and Littlehampton there were no problems as the tracks ran right along the quaysides.

The Changing Landscape

Mention has already been made of how the coastline has been artificially altered by man's devising, but the landscape has also visibly altered within the relatively brief period of the century embracing the photographs contained in this album, in particular by housing development. Many of what were once small villages and coastal towns have grown into vast conurbations, Brighton, for example, having extended its tentacles over the adjoining downland valleys, and the built-up area continuing right through to Shoreham. Popular resorts like Eastbourne, Bognor and Littlehampton have burgeoned into the hinterland, and areas like Bexhill and Worthing have swallowed up the neighbouring villages to provide bungalows and retirement homes along the coast. One has to go to the Kingscotes and Fittleworths in the heart of the countryside to capture the timeless beauty of the Sussex landscape so aptly described by Kipling, who was a Sussex poet:

> "Nor I don't know which I love the most,
> The Weald or the Marsh or the white chalk coast!
> I'm just in love with all these three,
> The Weald and the Marsh and the Down Countrie!"

A stopping train bound for No. 397's home base of Brighton pulls away from Hassocks. The train is entering the shallow cutting leading to Franklands Bridge. No. 397 of R.J. Billinton's D3 class emerged from Brighton Works in November 1896, and was one of just two selected by Earle Marsh for rebuilding with an I2 boiler involving the provision of a circular smokebox and saddle, a shorter chimney, closed dome, firebox-top Ramsbottom safety valves, a heightened cab and third coal rail to the bunker top. The condition of the locomotive indicates a picture taken not too long after the rebuilding date of June 1909. Note the line of stored lamps carried on the nearside tank cover.
H. Gordon Tidey/Lens of Sutton

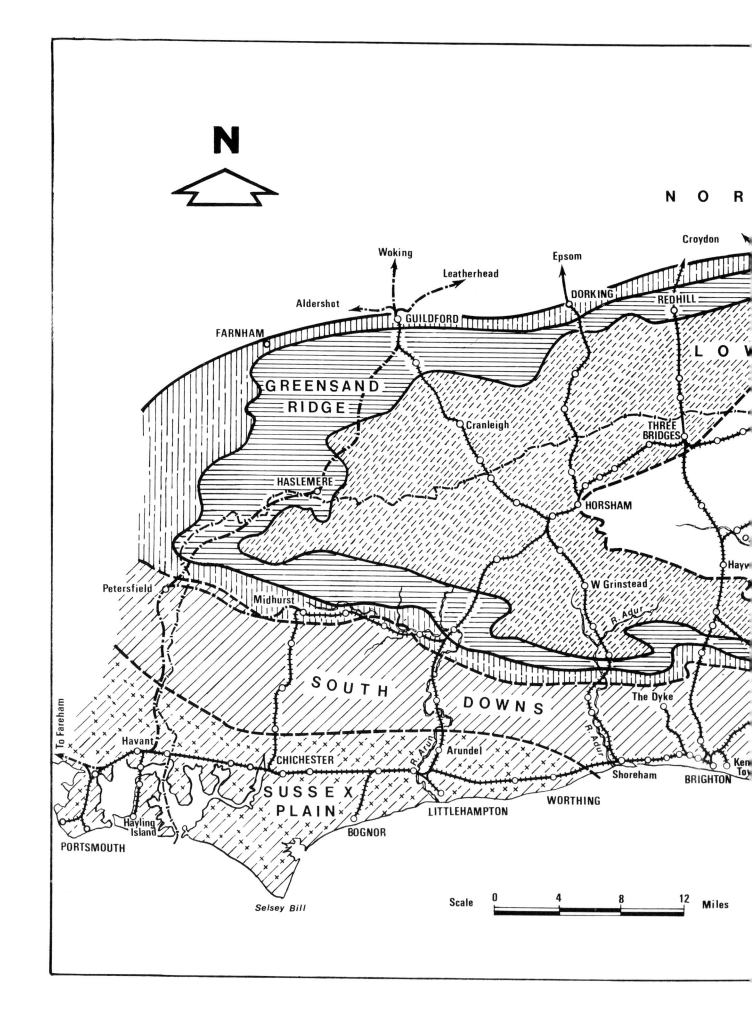

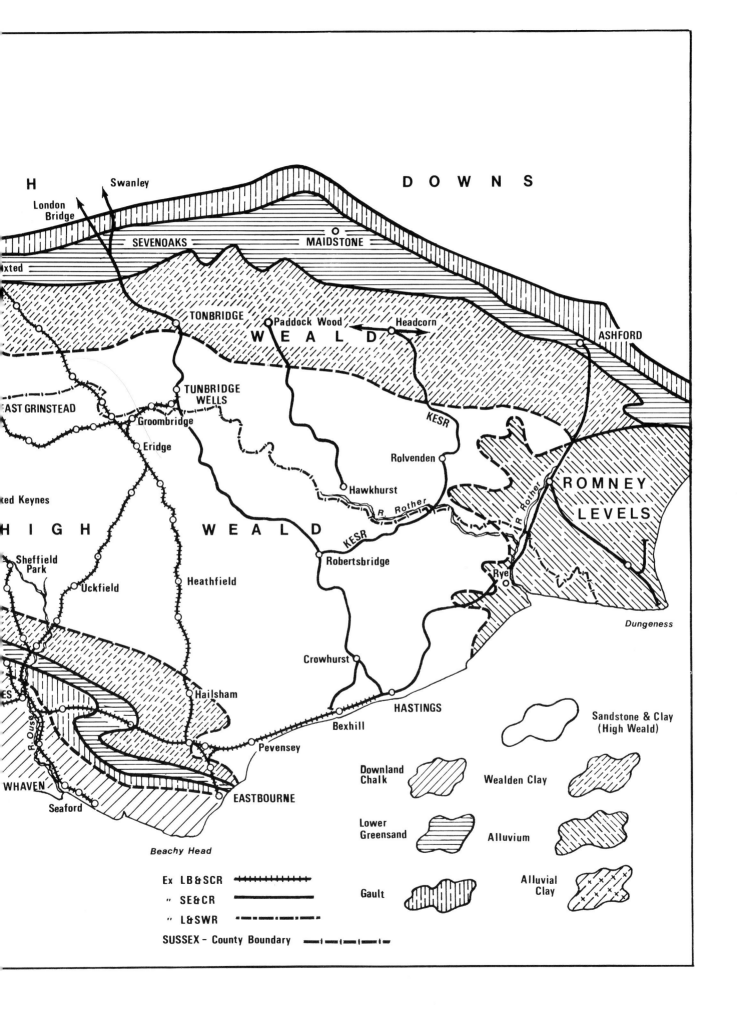

1　An unidentified 'Gladstone' and train at the eastern approach to Hove, receiving attention from an engineman at the front end. The date of the photograph is around 1890 when sleepers were still covered with ballast, and is full of interesting features (from left to right): the little white cabin, gas lamp, the East signal box – later Hove 'A' – framed by signals, and not least the majestic post at the end of the platform. The train has an ancient oil-lit passenger brake at each end. To the right of the locomotive is a decorative classical chimney and behind a glimpse of part of the original small station house designed by David Mocatta for the first station called Holland Road, which was open from May 1840 to March 1880. Further station structures were added in 1865 and 1893. On the bay loading platform stands a vintage covered truck belonging to Taylor's Depository. The line of housing hints at early urbanisation but the north side by the signal box still displays a rural appearance.
Lens of Sutton

THE WEST COAST LINE

2　The beginning of the end of steam in the Sussex landscape. At the close of 1962 a sad line of locomotives stands in Hove goods yard silhouetted against a carpet of snow, part of severe weather conditions typical of the 'big freeze' that winter which continued well into 1963. The built-up urban panorama of terraced housing and factory sheds is framed on the left by Hove 'B' signal box and on the right skyline by the floodlights of the Goldstone Ground. Hove yard is now the coal concentration depot for a wide area. The sudden withdrawal of such a large number of locomotives from the Central Section was thought to be part of an accountancy move to reduce the number of engines inherited by the British Railways Board. Nearest is K Class No. 32338 followed by E4 No. 32474, 'Schools' Class Nos. 30911 *Dover* and 30923 *Bradfield*, K Nos. 32341 and 32342, E6 No. 32417, E4 No. 32479 and E6 No. 32418.
E. Wilmshurst

3 The delightful combination of 'Terrier' and 'Balloon' coach on the Worthing rail motor has just passed under Olive Road bridge, close to Aldrington Farm, in 1906. The 'Balloon' rail motor carriages, first used with 'Terriers', belonged to a range of handsome vehicles which began to appear in 1905. They had much more headroom than previous LB&SCR carriages and their nickname was due to the very deep elliptical roof. There was a vestibule entrance and reversible seats in rattan with straphangers for those who had to stand. The motor train gear fitted to Nos. 81 and 82 was rod operated, passing under the rear buffer beam to the control trailer compartment. Earle Marsh's decision to convert the previously mentioned pair of 'Terriers' to 2-4-0Ts for the motor trains which commenced in September 1905 was shortlived, for the experiment proved unsuccessful, and No. 81 (formerly *Beulah*), seen here in umber livery with tank sides lettered LB&SCR, was re-converted to an 0-6-0T in 1907.

M.P. Bennett/Bluebell Archives

4 Scarcely a mile out of Hove, and not a building in sight amidst the wide open undeveloped fields. The scene is the shallow cutting beyond Aldrington with the cemetery enclosed by trees on the skyline. Photographed around 1906, E4 Class No. 486, already without its name *Godalming*, seeks to speed-up a westbound goods to keep clear of the next working on this heavily utilised section up to Shoreham. It includes four goods brakes in all, with a variety of wagons, several of them sheeted over their bars in true LB&SCR fashion. No. 486 was one of the first locomotives to lose its name when in 1905 Marsh, in the course of investigating a new livery, painted it glossy black with red and white lining and had the Company's initials substituted for the name on the side tanks. The black experimental livery was later rejected in favour of umber. *M.P. Bennett/Bluebell Archives*

5 An unidentified D Class tank locomotive sporting a replacement Billinton boiler and its immaculate Stroudley gamboge yellow livery leaves behind the houses of Portslade and is approaching a footbridge near Fishersgate from which the photographer is taking his picture. In the bottom left hand corner, part of the handrails to the stairs can be seen, to the right the approaching path. The seven coach set is of Billinton stock and every detail of the train and surrounding landscape has been picked out crystal clear in the coastal sunshine, whose glint has completely obscured the engine's name. Allotments, market gardens and ploughed fields recapture an idyllic scene that alas is no more, and Fishersgate Halt was opened in 1905, obliterating the railwaymen's allotments at this point.

M.P. Bennett/Bluebell Archives

6 Diminutive P Class 0-6-0T No. 31556 (preserved today on the Kent and East Sussex Railway) waits for some shunting to turn up at the sunlit harbour front at Kingston Wharf on 26th January 1959. The locomotive is standing at the foot of the 1 in 82 gradient built in 1938 to connect the wharf with sidings beside the main coast line. Prior to this date horses were used at both the head and foot of the incline. Wagons were connected by a chain to a stationary steam winding engine with turntables at either end. Originally there was a station at Kingston for steamship passengers to France when weather rendered the use of Brighton inadvisable, but this was closed in 1879 when the traffic was moved to Newhaven.

W.M.J. Jackson

7 An historic moment recorded by that renowned photographer of the LB&SCR, E.J. Bedford, of the last train across the old bridge over the River Adur at Shoreham on 8th June 1892. The passage of 'Gladstone' No. 186 *De La Warr* and its train of eight carriages and three passenger brakes, all oil-lit, captures the attention of not quite all the trio at work on the bridge that day. Officially known as Shoreham Viaduct and constructed in 1845, it was approached by a steep 1 in 80 ascent up the half mile from Shoreham. The Duke of Norfolk received compensation for two road toll bridges for loss of traffic; the one closest to the railway viaduct was purchased outright, and tolls were being collected more than a century later – by the Southern Region of British Railways. The river itself lies in a hollow at low tide screened by the mudflats and banks of sand and shingle.

E.J. Bedford/Bluebell Archives

8 'Battle of Britain' Pacific No. 34086 *219 Squadron* crosses the 1911 replacement bridge at Shoreham with a special transporting the Sadlers Wells Opera Company between Eastbourne and Bournemouth on 26th October 1963, late in the annals of steam workings on the Central Section but still at a time when locomotives could sport their nameplates and crests to the outside world. The River Adur, whose mud in the foreground and bank of shingle on the east side are clearly visible, was crossed by fourteen spans supported by iron columns. Passengers can obtain attractive views inland of the Adur gap, the rolling downlands and Lancing College Chapel, a well-known landmark.

P.J. Lynch

9 A regular weekday feature of this part of the West Coast line was the unofficially named 'Lancing Belle', which conveyed the considerable number of carriage works employees that lived in the built-up area around Brighton. Though Lancing was transformed by the railway from a sleepy little village, it was still only a small town even after the housing development that followed the construction of the works in 1912 on a sixty-six acre site to the south or coastal side of the railway. Various generations of workmen's coach sets using antiquated stock were provided over the years. Here, near the end on 20th April 1964, the uniformity of the six-coach set has been upset by the introduction of the experimental glass fibre bodied vehicle No. S1000 and a rear brake second of decidedly Maunsell vintage. The 7.10 a.m. from Brighton, indicating a long working day for its passengers, curves away from the main line across fields towards the heart of the works with Ivatt Class 2MT 2-6-2T No. 41314 in charge. Behind is a line of Lancing's more modern housing, while the soft curves of the downs inland stand out on the horizon. *E. Wilmshurst*

10 B4 Class No. 2051 has a motley collection of carriages in tow as it sets off from its Worthing stop, bound for Brighton in the early 1930s. The first vehicle is a Maunsell open third, a type under construction at this period and therefore relatively new. An electric train is standing in the down platform, doubtless destined for West Worthing, which was the limit of the live rail at that time. The short down platform was later extended when the West Coast line was electrified throughout in 1938.

Lens of Sutton

11 Another 4-4-0 ambling eastwards has a special working of empties from Cosham bound for Brighton. The formation includes a 'Lowmac' wagon at the rear! The locomotive is T9 Class No. 30283 of Eastleigh. Members of the class were frequent performers in the Southern period, and in post-war days were occasional visitors on workings coming on to the coast line from Hampshire. The scene is at Toddington on 18th March 1956, the train having just passed the site of the original Lyminster station of 1846 which closed in 1863 when the Littlehampton branch was opened. At the far left is the signal cabin which controlled the level crossing astride the Arundel–Littlehampton road.

E. Gamblin

12 A fascinating working passes the flats of the Arun river plain. Stroudley 'Terrier' No. 32640 (preserved at the time of writing on the Isle of Wight) has left the built-up area of Littlehampton behind as it heads north-west with a trainload of timber bound for Bognor on 6th May 1961. The location is the approach to a shallow cutting at exactly the halfway point of the 1¼-mile Littlehampton branch which divides at Littlehampton Junction, carrying straight on for Ford, or curving away for Arundel Junction, where the line again divides for the Mid-Sussex line and the West Coast line to Brighton. At this particular point on the Ordnance Survey map there is not a place name to be found for 1,000 yards in any direction.   *W.M.J. Jackson*

13 An electric unit berthing depot of three roads, together with partial colour light signalling, was installed on the Littlehampton branch as part of the SR Portsmouth No. 2 Electrification scheme which included the Mid-Sussex line and the remainder of the West Coast line. At the rear of the receding electric train is a 2-BIL unit, some of which were specially constructed for this scheme in 1938. N Class No. 31842 slows past the sheds on the approaches to Littlehampton with an inter-regional excursion consisting of stock of Great Western origin. The background provides another glimpse of the fertile Arun plain stretching to the distant downs, and includes a fine cluster of stalwart trees which have stood up well in this windswept area.   *E. Gamblin*

14 The two-road engine shed at Littlehampton dates back to the 1863 opening of the branch which terminates in the heart of the coastal town. It was soon surrounded by a built-up but not unattractive area, the delightful saintly looking police station on the left, together with the mid-Victorian, white-coated villas of Gloucester Road forming a vintage backcloth to the numerous photographic portraits taken of locomotives by the shed entrance or parked near the turntable (off picture on the left). By the date of this scene, 17th April 1938, this sub-shed to Bognor had been closed for a year, but still provided a turning and stabling point for the numerous steam locomotives requiring servicing. T9 Class 4-4-0 No. 336, stands awaiting its next turn. Behind it a pair of *ex*-LB&SCR tank locomotives are out of steam. The shed building survives as a parcels office and store.

K.O'B. Nichols

15 The LB&SCR developed a wharf at Littlehampton, obtaining Parliamentary powers to operate steamboat services: St. Malo, Jersey and Honfleur were among places served. In the late nineteenth century considerable farm and dairy produce was landed there, and it was a busy little port. However, when Newhaven was developed as the Company's principal port on the Sussex coast, Littlehampton lost its importance. It nevertheless played a vital role in both world wars. At the close of the 1960s the lines to the wharf were lifted to make way for a road to the new bridge upstream, though the port is still operational today but without rail connection. On 11th February 1956, with the wharfside and wagons carpeted in snow, 'Terrier' No. 32646 carries out its shunting duties. The locomotive has a lengthy and interesting history, preserved today on the Isle of Wight Steam Railway, being a former 'island' engine and having served as the 'Hayling Billy' inn sign on a plinth at Hayling Island.

E. Gamblin

16 This photograph of 'Merchant Navy' Class 4-6-2 No. 35007 *Aberdeen Commonwealth* leaving for Brighton with an RCTS/LCGB tour returning to Waterloo on 18th October 1964, provides a panoramic view of the railway at Littlehampton. From left to right are: the gasholder indicating the gasworks, 2-BIL units stabled on the electrified adjacent siding, behind the signal box the site of the former locomotive shed, and slightly to its right and on the south side of the station tracks, the tall two-road brick goods shed. Nearer the east bank of the Arun, is a water tower to avoid wharf shunters having to cross the station lines for replenishment; to the right foreground are sidings housing empty coal wagons and behind them the line to the wharf with its coal tips and cranes.

E. Wilmshurst

17 Littlehampton was one of the most popular of the Sussex coastal resorts, preferable to the working class patronage of Brighton, the snobbishness of Bognor Regis or the aristocratic refinement of Eastbourne. It was a favourite for children's excursions with the best sands in that part of Sussex and a mecca for day visitors. The coastal sky is still clear as Thompson B1 Class 4-6-0 No. 61329 pulls away from the town with the 6.53 p.m. return working to Chingford on London's eastern outskirts. Locomotive and stock have come through from the Eastern Region, and the ten coaches include some fine examples of Gresley's design. The date is 25th May 1957.

J.J. Smith

18 When the coastal lines had to cross rivers close to their estuaries, this posed considerable engineering problems for railway companies, for inland navigation in the mid-nineteenth century was still assumed to have the right of way at a time when the decline of river traffic had not yet set in. The answer was the construction of successive bridges over the River Arun of the bascule, swing and lift variety. Rebuilt B4X Class No. 2067 approaches the Arun Bridge in the mid 1930s with an excursion special, which includes a Pullman car bound for Bognor. The small, seemingly neglected cabin was there to serve the gang operating the bridge *Lens of Sutton*

19 B4X Class No. 2070 slows past the 'on' distant signal with a Cardiff–Brighton train *circa* 1938, with a very uniform set of mainly GWR compartment stock. The location is mid-way between Barnham and Ford, whose distant signals stand within a few dozen yards of each other along one of the few shallow cuttings in this part of the coastal flatlands. In the distance lies Todhurst Farm with its greenhouses and chimney of the boiler providing even heating throughout the day. The fact that much of the produce was uniquely grown under glass meant it could hold its own against housing in the fierce competition for land. *C.R.L. Coles*

20 An interesting westbound working approaches the platforms of Barnham Junction on 16th April 1938, double-headed by Marsh Atlantic tank engines, I1X Class No. 2598, a 1925 rebuild, and I3 Class No. 2026. Following the initial pair of Maunsell coaches is a rake of GWR coaches with roof boards suggesting that the Brighton–Cardiff through train has been strengthened with Southern coaches and a second locomotive. The immaculate concrete platform copings testify to the Southern Railway's extensive facelift and resignalling of the station in the late 1930s. The end of a newly-built 2-BIL unit on the right neatly frames the picture. Market gardens and fruit orchards stretch into the distance, the station with special covered loading facilities providing the focal point of the area's rail-borne horticultural traffic
K.O'B. Nichols

21 Photographs taken on the short 3½ miles-long Bognor branch are not plentiful, but this 1914 view of the west end of Barnham Junction Station shows 'Terrier' No. 650, still in unrebuilt condition, arriving with a train off the branch, hauling a diverse array of stock including a towering 'Balloon' coach and three passenger brake vehicles. The locomotive survives today as *Sutton* on the Kent and East Sussex Railway after a varied career including a stint on the Isle of Wight and in service stock as No. 515s at Lancing carriage works. It went back to line work on the Hayling Island branch until withdrawal in 1963, and was purchased by the Borough of Sutton and Cheam. Framed between the signal box and goods yard, and with the water tower and adjoining turntable partly screened by the train, the aspect westwards is flat and bleak for over a mile towards Woodgate and the London to Bognor road.
Lens of Sutton

22 The site of the former engine shed at Bognor was visible from the platforms. Only the LB&SCR water tower remained to service locomotives right through to the early 1960s. To the left foundations of the shed building and ashpit road (bereft of track) are clearly visible. The scene on 1st June 1957 shows, from left to right, unrebuilt Bulleid Pacifics Nos. 34092 *City of Wells* (still in existence today), 34068 *Kenley*, 34087 *145 Squadron* and 34017 *Ilfracombe* awaiting their working of return excursions to the London Midland Region. The station opened ninety-three years previously to the day. The single track was doubled by 1911 and Bognor acquired the suffix 'Regis' after King George V convalesced there in 1929.
E. Wilmshurst

23 Stroudley Single No. 344 *Hurstmonceux* stands with its 'double diamond' Goodwood Race special in the seeming heart of the countryside at the turn of the century. The expansive array of sidings, covered with a random sprinkling of ballast, today form part of the much rationalised Chichester yard. The stock on view provides a fine assemblage of Billinton six-wheelers, including the gleaming oil-lit passenger brake and, judging by the locomotive's shedcode of Battersea visible at the side of the front buffer beam, has obviously come all the way from London. The meadows in the background, known as Westgate Fields, are well watered by the River Lavant on its way to join the Chichester Channel, and provide a verdant foreground to a view of the cathedral which is off the picture on the right. *Bluebell Archives*

24 Chichester yard in 1951 with C3 Class No. 32303 on one of its last workings before withdrawal in September that year. Shedded at Fratton, it has arrived with a goods working from Hampshire which it is seen shunting back into the exchange sidings. The down sidings and most of the up ones have been lifted following the sharp decline in goods traffic from the wartime period when the Southern's trio of electric locomotives worked over the live rails into the nearest electrified reception road on the left. Chichester Station was modernised in 1957/8 with modern structures replacing the age-worn LB&SCR buildings, and it lost its bay platforms in a more recent track rationalisation. *C.R.L. Coles*

25 Drummond L12 Class 4-4-0 No. 418 leaves Chichester with an empty stock working of GWR coaches for Portsmouth. The date is 1946, just five years before its withdrawal. The panoramic view of Chichester and surrounds, seen from a convenient footbridge to the west of the station, includes from the left: part of the turning triangle laid down for locomotives that could not be accommodated on the 45ft. turntable; the entrance, behind the locomotive, to the reception sidings; further back the straggling up goods yard with its shed and cattle pens; the station still with its bay platforms and including some of the original 1846 buildings. Behind the signal box lie the former exchange sidings with the Selsey Tramway and, hidden from view, the turntable, with the gasholders and Sadler's tall warehouse prominent landmarks. The extensive down yard on the right was laid during the second world war and appears very busy, chock full of wagons compared to the reception sidings seen in the previous picture.

C.R.L. Coles

26 Thomas Oliver's construction train, *circa* 1880, working near the site of the future Singleton station: a portrait of the use of steam in altering the rural landscape. This posed picture is full of interest: the splendid variety of headgear displayed by the navvies, the diminutive spoil wagons necessitating the extra pair of dumb buffers on *Fred*, a Manning Wardle 0-4-0ST. Note the handy lengths of chain hanging from the buffer beam. Mr. Oliver of Horsham must have been a sub-contractor to Joseph Firbank who held the head contract for the line's construction. *D.E. Wallis Collection*

CHICHESTER TO MIDHURST

A twelve-mile single line over the downs between Chichester and Midhurst was always likely to provide formidable difficulties for a small independent company, crucially with regard to finance, and this soon proved the case with a start made in 1865 which had to be called off three years later. The dormant construction powers were taken up in 1876 by the LB&SCR which, incorporating the partly completed earthworks, opened the line on 11th July 1881. In a sparsely populated downland district, and involving three tunnels through chalk, the major attraction was Goodwood Racecourse. It was served by a grandiose station at Singleton equipped with two island platforms and sidings able to accommodate up to fourteen 20-coach trains, including Royal specials for King Edward VII. But once road transport arrived as a force to be reckoned with, the writing was on the wall, and passenger services ceased on 6th July 1935, one of the few early casualties and the first lengthy stretch of LB&SCR branch line to succumb. As with Kemp Town, goods services continued with successive reductions, the line today curtailing at Brandy Hole Lane siding serving a gravel pit. The line was very under-photographed as regards moving trains in the landscape, and those that exist have been frequently reproduced over the years. Proposals to reopen the southern end of the line as a tourist railway have so far come to nothing.

27 Lavant Station bears the stamp of the work of Joseph Firbank, similar style contemporary buildings being found on the 'Bluebell' and 'Cuckoo' lines constructed by the same contractor. Lavant is a mirror image of Newick & Chailey, being on three floors with the basement serving the platform, the middle storey the road frontage and the top serving as the station master's accommodation. From August 1953 the line was cut back to this point, Lavant becoming the railhead for the sugar beet traffic originating from the surrounding district. As a result the platform was strengthened and a run-round loop laid. C2X Class No. 32550 of Fratton shed waits to leave for Chichester yard with seven loaded wagons of sugar beet, its excess steam blurring the outline of Stoughton Down on the skyline.

S.C. Nash

28 Arundel lies at the point where the Arun valley opens out onto the coastal plain. Boats and barges used to come up to the town's wharf until fairly recent times, hence the former swing bridges further down towards the sea. When the railway came, a sizeable goods yard was provided and the river traffic soon dwindled; Littlehampton replaced Arundel as the area's principal port. The station is situated on the opposite bank to the town and castle, and lies in a leafy setting with the ridge of the downs to the north-west. The selection of wagons on view make this and similar photographs taken from the east side a mine of valuable information for analysis of the variety of goods traffic carried at the turn of the century on the LB&SCR system. The station itself is of grandiose proportions in keeping with the Duke of Norfolk's stipulations for the sale of land to the railway. The picturesque ivy-bedecked water tower not only has smoke drifting from the chimney but steam escaping from a pipe at the centre of the water tank, probably in connection with the pump house boiler. The locomotive is D Class 0-4-2T No. 10 *Banstead* waiting in the down bay in 1902 with a Littlehampton train. It was one of the earliest members of the class to go, being withdrawn only two years later. *Lens of Sutton*

THE MID-SUSSEX LINE

29 The station, which dates from 3rd August 1863, stands beside the main road to Worthing in a flat portion of the Arun valley with a splendid view of the historic town it serves. The locomotive is one of the revolutionary I3 class Atlantic tanks of the 1912 batch constructed after Marsh's retirement. The idea for this excellent design came in 1907 when, at the suggestion of his chief draughtsman B.K. Field, Marsh adopted superheated steam at a time when such a system was largely in its infancy. No. 82 is on a Portsmouth fast train in 1914, and is the centre of admiration for members of the station staff. Other points of interest are the LB&SCR horse boxes in the yard and a tall 'Brighton' signal at the rear, while the open guard's door of the coach in the bay platform indicates a connecting train for Littlehampton-bound passengers. *Lens of Sutton*

30 A C3 Class 0-6-0 No. 303, nicknamed 'Horsham Goods' by virtue of the class being represented at Horsham shed for the greater part of its working life, ambles a Horsham–Bognor goods along near Arundel in 1925. The valley gap northwards is on the horizon above the ubiquitous Stroudley brake van, while the valley shelves on either side complete the backcloth to the pastoral setting. While R.J. Billinton fitted his C2 class goods of 1893 with injectors, Earle Marsh reverted to Stroudley practice with the C3 class of 1906, using a Westinghouse feed pump. The rebuilding by Marsh of the C2s rather put the C3s into the shade, and they were relegated to less important and lighter tasks. No. 303 nevertheless has a tidy load to bring down the valley. *Lens of Sutton*

31 At almost the same scenic spot (note the crossover points and the white post on the left side of the track) B2X Class 4-4-0 No. 322, which lost its name *G.P. Bidder* when rebuilt in 1908, enters Arundel Station. It is captured in the lovely evening sunlit water meadows of the River Arun, patronised on the right by a herd of largely all-white cows. The refitting with C3 class boilers by Earle Marsh added an average of twenty more years to the members of the class. The train is a Portsmouth-bound fast comprising bogie stock. The extremely tall down home signal must have been visible quite a way up the valley, necessitated by the numerous tall trees by the lineside along the previous mile.

Bluebell Archives

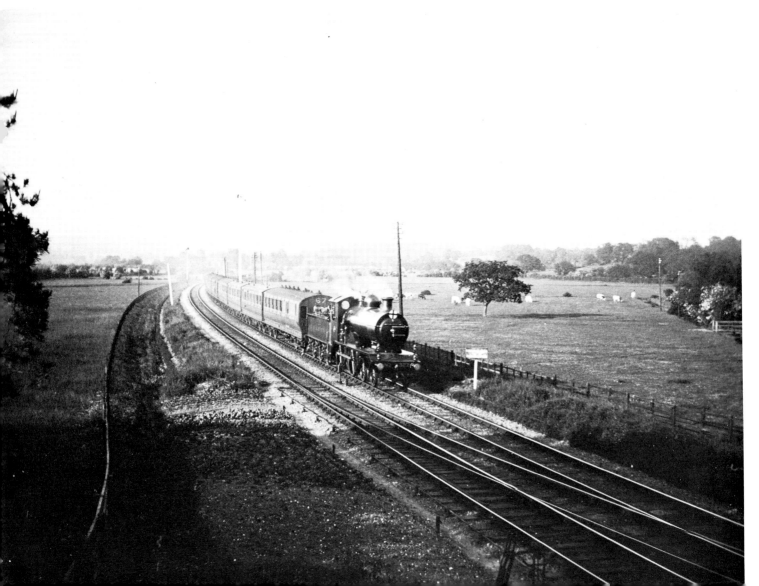

32 Cows are still in occupation almost half a century later at the same location with *ex*-LMS Stanier Class 5 No. 45288 approaching Arundel on 14th July 1957 working a Tring to Littlehampton excursion train composed of *ex*-LMS coaching stock. From this angle one can see more clearly the way the South Downs gradually climb to about 600ft beyond which they fall steeply near Amberley, making this area – which is generally inaccessible to road traffic – delightful walking country.

E. Wilmshurst

33 Following electrification in 1938 the number of steam workings on the Mid-Sussex line was drastically reduced and largely confined to infrequent goods trains. During its progress along the valley the railway crossed the River Arun on numerous occasions, the LB&SCR constructing new cuts for the Arun Canal and the winding river. This picture shows Q Class No. 30544, based at Horsham, in charge of the 4.24 p.m. Bognor Regis – Three Bridges goods on 1st June 1957, crossing the original (but now abandoned) route of the Arun at Burpham whose signal box can be seen towards the rear of the train. This flat river landscape with its profusion of tall reeds along its banks is typical of the Arundel – North Stoke section, with the downland about a mile from the line on each side. Today the Arun is used regularly in the summer months for commercial pleasure trips between Littlehampton and as far as Amberley. Not surprisingly there is a haven for wildfowl close by.

J.J. Smith

34   The year is 1937, shortly before electrification, for which the cabling on the left has already been installed. I3 Class No. 2085 slows for its stop at Amberley with the 4.46 p.m. Portsmouth Harbour – Victoria train on a pleasant high summer evening. In addition to the Maunsell 4-set, the rake is composed of a pre-grouping third, a passenger luggage van and a pair of horse boxes. The location is close to the hamlet of North Stoke, where a tunnel of that name was dug through a small section of downland.   *Lens of Sutton*

35   With Amberley Castle dimly visible on the skyline, D Class tank locomotive No. 268 brings its down stopping train across the Storrington to Arundel road which serves the station via an approach road. The year is 1914 and the rake of carriages a symmetrically-coupled Billinton set No. 56. Today the station at Amberley still retains a small signal box incorporated into the booking office on the down side. The entrance to the Chalk Pits Museum is a short walk from the station entrance; this attraction has boosted business at Amberley Station and on the line generally.   *Lens of Sutton*

36   A timeless ritual in the days of steam was the everyday scene of a locomotive taking water. In this pre-electrification picture, this delightful moment shows the final member of the I3 class standing at the head of a down stopping train in Pulborough Station on 16th April 1938. Besides being the last of the class to be constructed, No. 2091 was also the final survivor in service, lasting until May 1952. The roof of the subway stairs is under reconstruction, and amidst the general chaos at this point a rope is tied from the magnificent titular station board to a piece of piping by the subway brickwork.

K.O'B Nichols

37   An unusual working is seen proceeding at a leisurely pace northwards as Billingshurst Station and yard recede into the distance. The first E4 to be built in 1897, now masquerading as BR No. 32463, heads an Eastleigh – Three Bridges track-laying train homewards to its allocated base on 21st June 1959. The photographer appears to have been exceedingly fortunate to be in just the right place at the right time to obtain this picture of a very rare daytime movement, or maybe he was party to 'inside information'!

J.J. Smith

38 Exactly a week later and again 'in the know', and once more on a Sunday, the photographer has taken an out-of-the-ordinary engineers' special heading for Itchingfield Junction with a Barnham to Three Bridges working. The shallow sunlit cutting is enhanced by the presence of boys from the nearby Christ's Hospital School by the occupation crossing, a pleasant way of spending a Sunday afternoon. *J.J. Smith*

39 The line from Three Bridges to Horsham was one of the least photographed stretches of the Sussex railway system, in any case running close to the border with Surrey. The scenery was pleasant without being sensational, and electrification at the end of June 1938 rendered it even less appealing to steam photographers. Faygate Station, seen through the bridge in the distance, was original to the line which opened on 14th February 1848. An LMS-designed 2-6-2T No. 41301 (commonly known as a 'Mickey Mouse' tank) is on the 12.10 p.m. Horsham to Three Bridges van train on 6th April 1965, late in time for steam on the Central Section. A public footpath with accompanying notices adds interest to the scene.

J.J. Smith

40 Pulborough on 16th April 1938, showing newly installed trackwork and conductor rails. This was laid in connection with the Southern Railway's scheme to electrify the Mid-Sussex line which was announced in February 1936. Full electric services were introduced on 3rd July 1938, less than three months after this picture was taken. The branch to Midhurst remained steam-worked to the end which accounted in part for its early demise in 1955. M7 Class 0-4-4T No. 246, of Guildford shed, leaves in charge of one of the former L&SWR 'Gate' sets with a train bound for Petersfield. The interesting backcloth to the left is a garden nursery belonging to Cheals of Crawley, while the elaborate off-platform nameboard reads 'Pulborough for Petworth, Midhurst & C.'   *K.O'B. Nichols*

PULBOROUGH TO MIDHURST

41 Fittleworth was the first intermediate station on the line, and had a signal box which closed in 1931. The station was less than a mile from the village it served, opening in 1889, thirty years after the line. It was patronised in the early 1920s by the composer Edward Elgar who lived nearby in retirement. The age of the privately-owned car was to put the line out of business. This is only too well underlined here by the solitary passenger alighting from a Pulborough to Petersfield push-pull rail motor service on 27th May 1950. The lush wooded scenery belies the fact that the River Rother lies just a hundred yards to the left of the railway at this point.   *Pamlin Prints*

42 Q Class 0-6-0 No. 30530 returns to Pulborough with an LCGB/RCTS special train on 18th October 1964. This was the last passenger working to Midhurst and was composed of main line stock including a buffet car. It is seen passing close to Bigenor farm with the River Rother adjacent to the line behind the train. In the distance lie the heights of Flexham Park and Bognor Common, while Petworth is just out of sight behind the trees on the left.　　*G. Siviour*

43　Since 5th February 1955, when passenger services between Pulborough and Petersfield were withdrawn, goods services continued to run into Midhurst from the east until 18th October 1964. The line still saw several rail-tour specials, however, including this LCGB trip on 24th June 1962. It was hauled by a pair of LB&SCR Radial tank locomotives, E4 Class No. 32503 and E6 Class No. 32418, which have just passed Selham Station on their way to Midhurst. Selham goods yard, seemingly well patronised, remained in use until May 1963. The station buildings on the single platform, which still stand at the time of writing, were later taken over by a local farmer for the storage of agricultural items. Opposite was a single siding which served a cattle dock; this was approached by a separate roadway. The signal box controlling the siding was closed in the 1930s. Selham Station stood in an exposed and weatherbeaten spot serving a tiny hamlet, and intending passengers from surrounding villages, such as Graffham and Lodsworth, would have found Petworth or Midhurst rather more convenient. The locomotives at the head of the train were nearing the end of their careers: No. 32503 was one of only seven members of its class active at that time, and survived for a further nine months. The E6 class was down to three representatives at this point and little work remained for them. No. 32418 lasted a further six months, being condemned in December, 1962.　　*G. Siviour*

44　A final opportunity to ride the line between Pulborough and Petersfield was provided on 6th February 1955, the day following closure. The RCTS 'Hampshireman' rail-tour emerges from Midhurst Tunnel's western portal to enter the station. At its head are the last two representatives of class E5X, which were Marsh rebuilds in 1911 of R.J. Billinton's E5 class: no great improvement was, however, obtained. Both locomotives were based at Horsham shed; No. 32576 was withdrawn from traffic just over four months later while No. 32570 lingered till the following January. *Lens of Sutton*

45 The year is 1946, as M7 Class No. 328 stands with its single coach in the up platform, which accommodated Midhurst's 1881-built station building. The fireman attends to the coal flow in the bunker. The coach is a distinctive example, No. S3847S, which had a corridor along one side, but without the usual partitioning. An 'archway' separated each compartment, and passengers occupying seats at the ends of the coach had an uninterrupted view down the full length of the vehicle. Following withdrawal of the service on the line to Midhurst, No. S3847S appeared on the Lewes to East Grinstead line, where a token service was introduced after the legality of the original line closure had been called into question. Midhurst's railway development is a story in itself due to intense rivalry between the L&SWR and LB&SCR. The new station of 1881, built to accommodate the arrival of the line from Chichester, was of generous proportions with long platforms and canopies to match, and even boasted two separate single road engine sheds in pre-grouping days. The station area has now vanished under housing development.

R.A. Lissenden collection

46 The returning brace of class E5X Radial tank locomotives pass Rogate on 6th February 1955, having delivered 'The Hampshireman' rail-tour to a pair of L&SWR T9 class 4-4-0s at Petersfield. This working, apart from the demolition train, was the last movement across the Petersfield to Midhurst stretch. This was originally L&SWR territory, and is indeed the only section of L&SWR track to feature in this album. The county border with Hampshire is just over a mile from Petersfield and lies amongst the wooded horizon in our picture. The line is still in the heart of the Rother Valley and the flat landscape posed no real problems when the line was built in 1864. The station of Rogate and Harting was well over a mile from either village. The station houses along this part of the branch were built at right angles to the track, with other buildings parallel to them. Most buildings had their brickwork covered with plaster. By the date of this photograph the loop platform was disused, while the signal box, closed in 1932, was used as a ground frame for the goods yard. There was a brickworks a quarter of a mile beyond the Petersfield end of the station, with a private siding controlled by a ground frame.

Pamlin Prints

47 A Guildford-bound service in the low-lying clay vale of the River Arun coasts down the gradient of 1 in 130 towards Slinfold. Further west the grades were eased, at considerable additional cost, by order of the Board of Trade inspector who considered the 1 in 80 gradient originally laid for trains starting south from Rudgwick to be too severe. As a result, a special raised bridge was constructed over the original. The motive power was unusual and was short lived on this line, H Class 0-4-4T No. 31322 being stationed at Brighton shed during 1961 when this photograph was taken. The old LB&SCR enginemen were none too impressed with the *ex-L&SWR* M7s or former SE&CR H class locomotives, but by this date the native fleet of former LB&SCR tank locomotives had largely gone for scrap. *G. Siviour*

HORSHAM TO GUILDFORD

48 A volcanic smoke effect erupts from the chimney of *ex-L&SWR* 0-4-4T No. 30108 as it storms past the line of evergreen trees behind the north-west end of Slinfold's platform. The station, like the majority on the line, only served a small village, and with the road distance to Horsham being actually shorter than the railway's circuit via Christ's Hospital, traffic was never heavy. The yellow stuccoed station building blended delightfully with the landscape, and although the immediate vistas in the vicinity of the station were fairly constricted, many a passenger would have derived immense pleasure from the close up detail of the myriads of wild flowers on the grassy bank. The train is the 4.3 p.m. Horsham to Guildford, and the date 5th May 1956. *E. Gamblin*

49 More traditional motive power in the shape of former LB&SCR E4 Class 0-6-2T No. 32469, a class which held sway over the services from early Southern days till the closing years. The year is 1961 and the scene a Guildford-bound departure making a brisk start out of Slinfold. Even at this late period there are wagons in the yard, also such traditional items of railway equipment as a hand crane and loading gauge are to be seen. There was no passing loop at this station, and until closure to goods traffic in 1963 the signal box acted as a ground frame for the sidings. *G. Siviour*

50 The scene at Rudgwick with the morning Guildford to Horsham goods on 5th May 1956. The goods yard there was all that a country village could conjure up, embodying a wooden wagon turntable, seen between the solitary wagon and the buffer stop, which survived until the goods yard was lifted in the autumn of 1963. Wagons were moved by horse and with occasional human assistance in the form of a pinch bar levered between rail and wheel. The pick-up goods is in charge of C2X Class 0-6-0 No. 32523 of Horsham shed, a type which served the branch for more than half a century. *E. Gamblin*

51 Ivatt 'Mickey Mouse' 2-6-2T No. 41287 rolls into Rudgwick on a Horsham-bound train on 15th May 1965, against a pretty backcloth of rural foliage, in charge of Bulleid 3-set No. 818. A couple of minutes previously the train would have crossed the Surrey/Sussex border which runs over Baynards Tunnel. The platform awning is not the original, having replaced the traditional LB&SCR horizontal one soon after the second world war, and at this late juncture in the line's history has, together with the station house, been fully repainted. No. 41287 was to haul the last time-tabled service over the branch on Saturday 12th June 1965, the 7.34 p.m. from Guildford to Horsham.

T. Stephens

52 Four modes of transport feature in this photograph, namely road, rail, water and air. In the middle foreground is the main Shoreham–Steyning road, while the railway, along which an Ivatt 2-6-2T locomotive hauls the 8.19 a.m. Horsham to Brighton train on 15th July 1961, is clearly visible in the middle of the picture. It was the River Adur, however, which provided the first means of transport in the area for heavy goods, as it formed part of the Adur and Baybridge Navigation which once allowed barges to travel inland as far as Bay Bridge, near West Grinstead. The low-lying level area beyond the bridge is Shoreham Airport; a hanger is visible, but the terminal building is out of sight on the left. The trestle bridge, which was built in 1740, originally carried the Brighton–Portsmouth main road across the Adur, and a toll was levied on motorists for the privilege of crossing at that point. The whole area in the foreground has since been blighted by the Shoreham by-pass road bridge, and its associated intersections, which were constructed in the mid-1960s.   *E. Wilmshurst*

SHOREHAM TO HORSHAM

53 By 18th June 1955, when all but one of the regular D3s on the line had been withdrawn from traffic, members of the E4 class based at Brighton took over the services. No. 32514 has almost completed its journey over the appositely named 'Linger Line', and is doing just that as it sidles past Old Shoreham, photographed against the stark bare slopes of the South Downs.   *E. Gamblin*

54 D Class 0-4-2T No. 297 is captured entering Steyning from the south, shortly after resuming passenger duties in 1906, following a spell as the Brighton paint shop pilot and losing the name *Bonchurch* on going through works. The train consists of Stroudley four-wheelers, except for the leading Billinton double ended luggage van. In the side of the cutting is an 'Advertising Station' (as groups of lineside hoardings were called in those days) under the name of Harman Davey. Advertisements for Tennants lager beer, Johnnie Walker whisky and Hartley's marmalade show products have not changed all that much in the meantime.

M.P. Bennett Collection/Bluebell Archives

55 Steyning was a port in medieval times until the banks of the River Adur were built-up in Elizabethan days, a fact borne out in living memory when the sea reached and flooded low-lying parts of the town in the winter of 1924/5. The station scene depicted near the end of its days had on display five ever-decreasing items of 'railway furniture', namely the signal box, semaphore signal, water crane, loading gauge and goods shed. Ivatt 2-6-2Ts were only associated with the line during the final years of steam working. No. 41261, minus shedplate but obviously an import from another Region, resumes its journey with a Horsham-bound train on 6th August 1961. Two months later the station was the venue for local celebrations of the line's centenary with a special train hauled by E4 Class No. 32468 while A1X 'Terrier' No. 32635, the former Brighton Works shunter, was on display in the goods yard. From 3rd May 1964 passenger services were operated by diesel-electric multiple units, but the line nevertheless succumbed on 5th March 1966. *S.C. Creer*

56 Leaving behind the South Downs on the horizon, but not the River Adur which the line has crossed and recrossed since leaving Steyning, M7 Class 0-4-4T No. 30051 shuts off steam as it coasts into Partridge Green with an up train, bound for its home depot of Horsham. These *ex-L&SWR* products received mixed comments from the local enginemen when they arrived on the Central Section in the early 1950s. They did not begin to leave their Sussex bases till after 1960, so cannot have performed that badly. They were adequate workhorses for the branch line tasks and, judging by the lack of paint on the smokebox side, not unwilling to extend themselves, though the line had only moderate grades and light passenger loads which did not overtax locomotives.

G. Siviour

57 West Grinstead with its towering pines was as pretty a station setting as one could choose, while down at the side of the cutting clusters of primroses can be discerned in this April 1960 photograph of a southbound train accelerating from its station stop. E4 Class No. 32503 of Brighton looks in good trim and was one of the last of the class to be withdrawn exactly three years later. The leading vehicle is a Maunsell Brake converted for push-pull operation. West Grinstead station differed from others on the line in that the main buildings were above the tracks at road level, beside the bridge carrying the A272 Haywards Heath–Billingshurst road over the railway. Station passenger receipts were very modest, its location being isolated from even small centres of population.

G. Siviour

58 Steam in the Sussex landscape *par excellence*: an aesthetic portrait which includes a superb backdrop of corn stools betokening the 1960 harvest. The train making its sedate way south is the 5.0 p.m. Horsham–Brighton empty coaching stock working, consisting of two local sets each made up of a Maunsell 2-coach push-pull set plus an additional pre-grouping third. The locomotive is C2X 0-6-0 No. 32535 in a much less polished condition than when it ran the pioneer Bluebell RPS special the previous summer. The location is north of West Grinstead.

G. Siviour

59 Another C2X, No. 32527, heads back from the coast for its home base at Three Bridges. Slotting such a goods working between speedy electric services on the two-track section of the Brighton main line was to be avoided, and so the less busy path over the Steyning line was a useful alternative. It has just passed through Southwater, whose down platform is visible behind the guards van. The white cottage screens the station buildings but the crossover and crossing boards can just be discerned. An alternative route between the platforms was via the A24 roadbridge. The delightful rustic cottages behind the field on the left appear through the wisps of smoke and steam.

J.H.W. Kent

60 A vintage LB&SCR-style branch train powers round the curve which takes the Steyning line away from the Mid-Sussex route at Itchingfield Junction, whose signal box is wreathed in drifting smoke. At least two serious accidents, one in 1866 and another in 1964, have occurred near this point, both involving fatalities. The R.J. Billinton D3 0-4-4Ts were the mainstay on this line in the immediate post-war years, leaving child-hood memories for one of the authors of kindly drivers not averse to consenting to footplate rides between Christ's Hospital and Holland Road Halt, away from the prying eyes of inspectors at Horsham and Brighton! No. 32376 is in charge of the 5.19 p.m. Horsham–Brighton on 24th May 1952, and had exactly one remaining year ahead of it. *J.J. Smith*

THE KEMP TOWN BRANCH

61 Turn of the century Kemp Town, as Stroudley 'Terrier' No. 63 *Preston* pauses while the points are changed to enable it to run round its Stroudley high capacity close-coupled suburban set. From 1906, a half-hourly rail motor service was introduced to meet local competition from electric tram cars. Chances of success were greatly reduced by the wartime closure between 1st January 1917 and 10th August 1919, during which the traffic transferred to the roads, never to return to the railway. In the distance stands the ornate portal of the tunnel with the signal box to the left of the entrance, set against the towering chalk face cut to make room for an extensive goods yard served by horse-drawn two-wheeled private owner carts. Above it, housing development has crept extremely close to the cliff top, the rear gardens providing a panoramic view of the whole station area and the sea just beyond. The date of the photograph is before June 1901 when *Preston* went on the duplicate list to become No. 663. *M.P. Bennett/Bluebell Archives*

62 A former SE&CR D Class 4-4-0, reckoned to be amongst Wainwright's finest designs, *ekes* out its closing days on a modest local transfer trip, the 10.48 a.m. from Brighton Top Yard to Brighton East Goods Depot, at Kemp Town. The locomotive is just about to cross the three-arch viaduct over Hartington Road, while further back along the curve are the arches of the longer Lewes Road viaduct. The backcloth is indicative of the total urban development of the downland ridges around Brighton. The date is 12th March 1955, just six months before No. 31734 was retired with an impressive mileage of 1,427,156 and stored at Ashford for possible restoration. However, its frames and cylinders were found to be defective and later No. 31737 was chosen to represent this famous class in the National Collection, now housed at York. *J.J. Smith*

63 The 1 mile 32 chains-long branch closed to passenger traffic at the end of 1932 when the Brighton main line was electrified. In post-war years the line saw a number of special passenger workings, one of which ran over the branch on 28th September 1958. This was the 12.47 p.m. empty stock working comprising a C2X Class 0-6-0 No. 32449, pleasantly turned out by its home shed of Brighton, together with a Maunsell brake *ex*-Set No. 261 plus an *ex*-SE&CR 'Birdcage' 3-Set No. 620. This train has come off Hartington Road viaduct and is seen passing the site of the short-lived Hartington Road Halt of which no visible trace remains. It was only open for five years, being closed at the beginning of June 1911. The location presents one of the few more open, almost rural spots on the branch, before the single line plunges into the 1,024 yards-long Kemp Town tunnel. *J.J. Smith*

64 The Dyke, for all its glamour, was not the most wonderful of places on bleak days when the low lying clouds clung to the downs and mist enveloped the complete panorama. Such dour conditions did not deter the photographer from recording the train guard in full regalia with straps and polished clasps and badges, posing with his little boy (also displaying brass buttons) beside the smokebox of E4 Class No. 484 *Hackbridge*. Entering service in April 1899, it was based at Brighton from the following year with hardly any interruptions through to the grouping. The year is 1907, and the occasion a snatched moment in the course of running round its train. An E4 at this early date is unusual at the Dyke, the Edwardian services being very much in the hands of Stroudley D tank locomotives and the occasional E1 class 0-6-0T. It is a picture full of interest, with curious onlookers in addition to the footplate crew. The figure holding a framed plate glass negative near the platform lamp post is one of the Bennett brothers who were amateur railway photographers of their day. The light has caught the wheels and motion of *Hackbridge* to perfection. *M.P. Bennett/Bluebell Archives*

THE DYKE BRANCH

65 The classic view of the Dyke terminus photographed from the lane winding up to the summit has been repeated many times, but this particular shot is more sharply focused than most, showing the station buildings and furniture in good detail – the station approach path with its enamel advertising signs, a grounded wagon body nudging the fencing, while behind, a storage shed and permanent way hut provided a degree of shelter in rough weather. The corrugated iron station building with its adjacent and attractive signal cabin, platform seats and lamp posts, add a civilising touch to the otherwise bleak expanse of the smooth downlands, scarred only by the chalk cutting and hedged and fenced lineside, receding in a huge S-shaped curve into the distance. The locomotive in attendance with its 'Balloon' coach is a Stroudley D tank, one of those renumbered into the 600 series and carrying the Southern Railway's shining new green livery. *Bluebell Archives*

66 Another murky day at Dyke station as an unidentified E4 Class 0-6-2T, standing beside the run-round loop, unloads an extremely optimistic group of excursionists at the solitary platform of the terminus. Tickets are inspected and collected before the day trippers begin the brief but stiff climb to the hotel restaurant at the summit viewpoint. There may not have been much to see on that occasion, but they say the downland ozone was always well worth the journey. Weather apart, this picture, taken in the immediate post-1923 grouping period before the Southern Railway had got round to putting their livery on to the locomotive, indicates a fair degree of patronage with the 'Balloon' brake trailer supplemented by a pair of pre-grouping thirds.   *Lens of Sutton*

67 A closer view of 'Balloon' trailer No. 3829 in Southern livery as E4 Class No. 2505 departs from the Dyke, part of whose 300 ft-long platform can be seen on the left. Behind the further signal is the bay in which goods vehicles were frequently parked for unloading. In the background Dyke Farm and sundry cottages stand in the fields which slope up to the summit ridge, and the roof of the Dyke restaurant can be discerned directly above the curve of the bay siding. No. 2505 operated on the branch during its final seasons and in fact hauled the very last train on the closing day of December 1938.

O.J. Morris/Lens of Sutton

68 Brighton MPD was the motive power hub servicing the bulk of locomotives throughout the county as lines radiated from the vast southern terminus on an arc from east round to west. Set in a landscape largely of bricks and mortar, only the trees grouped around an open field – seen behind the roof of the electric multiple unit inspection shed to the rear of the depot – remain of what a century ago was a vast expanse of green and parkland astride the Preston Road, which the line crossed to the east on David Mocatta's magnificent London Road viaduct of 1846. Even the large site of the engine shed witnessed a transformation in the mid-nineteenth century, requiring the total removal of a chalk hill, of which only a part had been cut into when the pioneer section to Shoreham was opened in 1840. This classic view of the shed scene has been taken from a wall at the top of the nearside chalkface, scaled and crested by the aptly named Terminus Road. The date is 5th October 1952, when E4 No. 2485 in the foreground still carried its Southern number. Coded 75A, the entire shed complex closed in June 1964 and was subsequently demolished, and today the site is occupied by an engineering depot. *D.B. Clayton*

THE BRIGHTON LINE

69 The scene overlooking the north end of Brighton terminus on 18th September 1966 with the world-famous L&NER A3 Class Pacific No. 4472 *Flying Scotsman* entering with a special train organised by Locomotive Preservation (Sussex) Ltd., an obscure organisation active at that period in running tours in the south of England. The train ran from Victoria, and later traversed the West Coast line to Salisbury, returning to London via Hove. On the left lies the neck to the former MPD; over on the right the vast covered area comprising Brighton Works which was swept away in the next decade to make way for a car park. The signal box and footbridge were the most recent to go in the 1985 Brighton resignalling scheme. *J.H.W. Kent*

70   To pacify the residents of Worthing and the fast-growing resort of Cliftonville (today's Hove), a direct line was constructed leaving the main line just south of Preston Park and avoiding Brighton Station altogether. The Cliftonville spur was opened on 1st July 1879 and included a 535 yards-long tunnel which was almost straight, the curves coming at each end of the cut-off line. M7 No. 30055 is seen emerging from the east portal with an empty stock working. It was possible to turn round whole trains on the triangle of lines completed by this spur, and also locomotives at times of great pressure in the shed yard. Note the high sloping retaining walls built to check chalk erosion.

J.H.W. Kent

71   Loosely termed the 'American Pullman' by its patrons, the officially named 'Pullman Limited' headed by one of William Stroudley's 'Gladstone' Class 0-4-2s still seems in a hurry at this late stage of the journey from London to achieve a right-time arrival at Brighton with less than a mile to go. This early 1890s picture (note the ballast covered tracks) illustrates the composition of this luxury train, the cars *Victoria*, *Beatrice*, *Princess of Wales*, *Duchess of York* and *Her Majesty* (familiar names today), being sandwiched between a pair of Pullman 'Pups', used for baggage and housing the batteries for the electric carriage lighting. Note the old slotted-post signals, and, behind the train, the tree covered chalk bluff of Tongdean.

Bluebell Archives

72 A post-grouping view taken from the other side of the tracks with 'Remembrance' Class 4-6-4T No. B328, as designed by Lawson Billinton in 1914, covering the last stages into Brighton with an express consisting of a mixed array of pre-grouping stock, a SE&CR 'Birdcage' set prominent near the front. The locomotive was rebuilt to an N15X class 4-6-0 in 1936, and was withdrawn at the beginning of 1955. The lines from left to right are: the pair of Cliftonville spur lines, the up and down main lines and, on the far side, a down loop line which also led to Brighton goods depot. The tall signals on view have arms which control roads to sidings at Preston Park, the up loop and up main. The box serving the south end of Preston Park Station was demolished during the Brighton resignalling scheme of 1985.
Lens of Sutton

73 The K class Moguls, though designed specifically for heavy goods work, could, when pressed, turn their hand to any task assigned by the shed foreman. The locomotive in the photograph is one of seven members of the class which had the Billinton top-feed housed in a second dome. It carries the original cab, though later all had the cab roof altered to suit the composite gauge and were fitted with flat topped domes. The class was superheated and the first on the LB&SCR to be constructed with Belpaire fireboxes. The train consists of a fine selection of antiquated 'Brighton' carriages which make up a return excursion for London, accelerating on the up main through Preston Park. Through the smoke in the distance loom the terraced slopes of the former chalk downland spur which separated the Preston Valley from the coastland at Hove. *Lens of Sutton*

74 Passing the north box at Preston Park with a fine overall view of the station is 'King Arthur' Class 4-6-0 No. 799 *Sir Ironside*, one of a batch of Southern Railway-built express engines drafted in to cope with the gap left by the rebuilding of the former Brighton Baltic tank locomotives in the handling of the principal Central Section expresses prior to the 1933 electrification. Nos. 793–806, carrying Ashford 3,500-gallon six-wheeled pattern tenders, were posed no problems on the shorter mileages from London to the south coast. The train provides a splendid mix of LB&SCR stock on view including, under the tall platform starting signal, a couple of Marsh elliptical coaches and, further back, two Pullman cars. *Lens of Sutton*

75 The B2 class, built to replace Stroudley G class 2-2-2s on the Portsmouth line, performed disappointingly and would have been assigned to the scrapheap after hardly more than ten years in service, had they not been rebuilt with Marsh C3 boilers. No. 317 was one of the first to be so treated in October 1908, and the converted B2X class were quickly put on the front line work. The condition of the locomotive would seem to indicate use immediately after rebuilding, before No. 317 was returned to its home base of Portsmouth. The service is a crack express to London comprising three of the American style Pullman cars followed by a set of Marsh main-line stock. The train is bursting out of the first, and shorter, of the two downland tunnels, which burrows under the grounds of Patcham Place, an unusually heavily wooded scarp. The bridge parapets belong to the road to Hove which avoids Brighton by climbing round the back of the downs through West Blatchington. *Lens of Sutton*

76 Photographs taken of up trains on the east side of the line are rare due to the position of the sun and lack of vantage points. The mound of earth on the right was probably a relic of the contractor's earthworks and was known to the enthusiast fraternity as 'The Plateau', a good vantage point in steam days. The train is climbing away from Patcham Tunnel on a grade of 1 in 264 which is maintained all the way to Clayton Tunnel. The locomotive is from the second batch of six Marsh Atlantics built in 1911 at Brighton Works. In 1925 the Southern Railway's Publicity Department enhanced their status by assigning them names. Here with plenty of steam in hand No. 32421 *South Foreland* accelerates dramatically towards London with the 8.48 a.m. Hastings–Wolverhampton (Low Level) holiday working which has reversed at Brighton. The date is 27th August 1955, exactly a year prior to the locomotive's withdrawal. The H2s owed their long post-war survival to such workings – there was little to occupy them in the winter months.

J.H.W. Kent

77 A most rare visitor to Brighton appeared in the shape of an *ex*-LM&SR 'Jubilee' Class 4-6-0 paired with a Fowler tender. No. 45595 *Southern Rhodesia* unusually carries a crest above the barely discernible nameplate. The photographer noted that the tender was leaking badly at Brighton and had to be topped up frequently to prevent it running dry. The train, the 12.30 p.m. Hastings–Manchester (London Road), looks longer than it really is, for a down e.m.u. is about to enter the 492 yards-long Patcham Tunnel. This location is now the site of a major Brighton by-pass road, and everything except the railway and the accompanying lineside flora on view has been obliterated. *J.H.W. Kent*

78 With the bluff of Patcham Place still in view, K Class Mogul No. 32343, based at Brighton, heads northwards with the Sunday 12.34 p.m. Bognor Regis–Victoria vans on 22nd July 1956. The working was presumably diverted due to engineer's occupation on the Mid-Sussex line. The A23 lies screened by the trees that have sprung up on the downland chalk over more than a century following the railway excavations. To the right and westward the surface carries its more traditional downland covering. *J.J. Smith*

79 Heading north the main line climbs gently into the heart of the South Downs, mostly in deep chalk cuttings, here well grassed-over by the passage of time. This attractive picture was taken in 1909 from a farm occupation overbridge near Scare Hill, carrying a lane from the main parallel London–Brighton road, a mere stone's throw away behind the ridge on the right. It shows a Victoria–Brighton express of Marsh elliptical stock in the short-lived umber and white livery, the fourth and fifth carriages being Pullman cars, and at the head Marsh Atlantic No. 38, one of the initial pair which were delivered by Kitson & Co. at the end of 1905. The five members of this first batch quickly took charge of the fastest expresses. *M.P. Bennett/Bluebell Archives*

80   The turn of the century was the period *par excellence* of seaside excursions, and each summer weekend would witness a succession of specials steaming down the main line to the various coastal resorts, especially those west of Brighton which boasted sandier beaches. G Class 2-2-2 No. 333 *Ventnor* heads a Littlehampton-bound excursion special, denoted by the 'double diamond' headcode in front of the chimney. The train has just cleared Clayton Tunnel and is passing over a section of track which is in the course of being relaid, as indicated by the array of rail lengths between the two tracks and the sleepers deposited near the bottom of the side of the imposing chalk cutting, still very much in its pristine splendour. The discerning reader will just be able to pick out the small signal cabin by the left of the tunnel mouth with its accompanying flights of stairs providing access for the signalman to the main road which runs just behind the chalk face above the tunnel entrance. *Ventnor* was withdrawn in November 1908.   *M.P. Bennett/Bluebell Archives*

81   The same view some sixty years later of another coast-bound excursion train of more recent times, in this case a Sunday excursion from Nuneaton to Brighton on 6th August 1961. The designated locomotive, carrying an LMR-style reporting number on its smokebox door, is Stanier 'Black Five' 4-6-0 No. 45416, just out of works. This closer view of the tunnel mouth shows more clearly the lengthy set of wooden stairs ascending the cutting-side to the left. The signal box has gone, and scrub and bushes have established a firm hold over the sides of the deep chalk cutting. The hamlet of Pyecombe, its chief importance as a downland junction of several roads, lies immediately above the tunnel, while to the right of the large house is the first of the tunnel ventilation shaft towers that indicate the line of the railway below to the passing motorist on the A273.

S.C. Creer

82　The glorious sweep of Clayton cutting as the line from Brighton burrows into the heart of the downland escarpment. N Class Mogul No. 31829 passes the isolated signal box at the head of the 10.20 a.m. Hastings–Sheffield Victoria on 27th August 1955. This train ran via the Great Central line calling at Woodford Halse (3.10 p.m.), Rugby (3.32 p.m.), and then via Leicester Central and Nottingham Victoria to arrive at Sheffield at 5.54 p.m. Just beyond the rear of the train, which includes several Gresley and Thompson coaches in its formation, is an electricity sub-station distributing current to this section of the Brighton main line. In the background are the downland slopes leading up to the Devil's Dyke which, viewed from this direction, lies just beyond Saddlescombe.　　*J.H.W. Kent*

83　David Mocatta's embellishment of the north portal of Clayton Tunnel remains a talking point amongst railway historians to this day. It has been suggested that the castellated entrance of the LB&SCR's longest tunnel of 2,266 yards was to reassure nervous people in open third class carriages that, although they were about to be borne underground through a massive ridge of chalk, their means of transit was entirely substantial and would not collapse on to them! The dwelling house between the two towers was probably built for the use of the man who had to look after the gas lighting inside the whitewashed cavern. Emerging from the darkness is N Class 2-6-0 No. 31812 of Stewarts Lane with a return holiday train from the coast bound for Sheffield, Gresley coaching stock well to the fore, on 6th August 1955. Note in the distance behind the left tower the northern-most tunnel vent; at the time of building, 1838/9, as many as eleven shafts were sunk to ventilate and assist the excavations.
J.H.W. Kent

84 Sister engine No. 31811 on an identical working later in the same month is seen powering away from Clayton Tunnel in a fine slipstream of smoke, and approaching the farm occupation track overbridge leading to Butcher's Wood. The background includes a panoramic view of the downland ridge and, by the A273 road to Burgess Hill, the 'Jack and Jill' public house named after the well known pair of windmills just out of the picture on the left. Note when comparing the two photographs the 'slipped disc' below the 73A Stewarts Lane shedplate which seems tied by unorthodox means to the buffer beam of No. 31811. *J.H.W. Kent*

85 L Class No. 1780 looks comfortably in charge of a High Wycombe–Brighton excursion of GWR stock on 30th June 1935. A year earlier this *ex*-SE&CR class might have been singled out as a rare visitor to the Southern Railway's Central Section, but the merger in July 1934 of the two Battersea sheds under one roof at Stewarts Lane saw the class make regular appearances in Sussex. Behind the train lies Hassocks Station with goods shed and water tank prominent, and at least two other trains within the station precincts.
LCGB Ken Nunn Collection

86   In the early evening light the final survivor of the famous class of three dozen 'Gladstone' 0-4-2s, No. 172 (formerly *Littlehampton*) approaches Hassocks Station with the 4.8 p.m. Brighton–London Bridge on 19th May 1932. Through the smoke haze and diffused sunlight the South Downs stand silhouetted, briefly broken by the V-shaped gap of the road past Clayton. In its final years before withdrawal in September 1933 No. 172 appeared on a wide range of services on both the main line and 'Sunday League' excursions. It made the headlines on 13th August 1931 on an exceptionally heavily-loaded Victoria to Bognor and Littlehampton express consisting of twelve crowded bogies, and the veteran in its closing days acquired the following of a film star, its demise mourned by railwaymen and enthusiasts alike.   *Lens of Sutton*

87 A view just south of Burgess Hill as 'West Country' 4-6-2 No. 34046 *Braunton*, one of a batch of five light Pacifics stationed at Brighton in the 1950s, pulls out the stops as it takes the 11.5 a.m. Walsall–Hastings train up the final stage of the rising gradient towards Clayton Tunnel on 28th August 1954. The stock is from the London Midland Region. The tracksides are framed by wild flowers enjoying the height of summer.

J.H.W. Kent

88 Stroudley G Class Single No. 331 *Fairlight*, sporting a splendid array of headcode discs including a 'double diamond' at the foot of the chimney, slows – note that only one 'peg' is off on the junction signal – for the sharp curve at Keymer Junction with a lengthy special for Hastings in early Edwardian days. There had been a severe crash at this point in 1899. Though Robert Billinton considered the class still had an important part to play and fitted most with new boilers and fireboxes as well as supplying several sets of cylinders, Earle Marsh took the opposite point of view and commenced withdrawal in mid-1907. *Fairlight* went in February 1909 and the class were all gone before the outbreak of the 1914 war. The northern approach to the junction lies in a shallow cutting with Wivelsfield Station and signal box behind the rear of the train, serving the adjacent hamlet named Worlds End. *M.P. Bennett/Bluebell Archives*

89 This photograph was taken on the same day but almost two miles further north; the location is Ashenground bridge looking towards the buildings of Haywards Heath along the skyline. The tracks lead up to the tunnel at Haywards Heath, the late winter Wealden scenery being chiefly leafless silver birches and evergreen pine trees. H1 Class Atlantic No. 41 has the Pullman Limited well in hand on its just over fifty-mile run to Brighton scheduled for an hour or, to be exact, fifty-nine minutes, for trains left Victoria a minute after the advertised starting time.

M.P. Bennett/Bluebell Archives

90 The end of steam on the Southern Region was less than four months away on 12th March 1967 when ex-L&NER K4 Class No. 3442 *The Great Marquess*, restored to its former livery, hauled a Waterloo–Lymington Pier special organised by Locomotive Preservation (Sussex) Ltd. It is seen approaching Haywards Heath from the north through Copyhold cutting over trackwork rationalised by BR following the closure of the Horsted Keynes branch beyond Ardingly. The single track through the right hand arch of Copyhold Bridge was deemed sufficient for the traffic to and from the roadstone plant at Ardingly and operates as an extended siding. Silver birch saplings again dominate the cutting sides; in the right foreground a start has been made on cutting back the intense lineside growth that quickly springs up if left unattended for more than a few years.

J.S. Everitt

91 The scenic view of the Sussex heartlands rising towards Balcombe Forest, seen on the skyline behind the tall LB&SCR distant signal, is taken from the bridge at Copyhold seen in the previous picture. This lies astride the junction of the branch from Horsted Keynes and Ardingly, opened in 1883, and the Brighton main line, down which B2 Class No. 209 *Wolfe Barry* heads a coast-bound express. The first two coaches in the formation are of Set No. 17, the third a Pullman Car. No. 209 emerged from Brighton Works in 1897 and was not rebuilt to class B2X until the spring of 1913. During most of this time it was stationed at Hastings, the depot being sited at St. Leonards. The line to Ardingly curves away through the grounds of Rivers Farm while the line of trees beyond marks the line of the ill-fated Ouse Valley Railway of 1864–7.

M.P. Bennett/Bluebell Archives

92 Framed in the inner pavilion arch on the south-west corner of the Ouse Valley Viaduct is the previously mentioned special hauled by No. 3442 *The Great Marquess*. The K4 class 2-6-0 was built for the West Highland line in 1937, and turned out to be one of the first privately preserved locomotives in the United Kingdom, being purchased by the late Lord Lindsay (then Viscount Garnock) in 1962. The crossing of the main tributary stream of the Ouse presented the London and Brighton Railway with one of its greatest challenges. The viaduct has stood the test of time well, although the stonework in this rare close-up view of the structure certainly appears stained with age and has tufts of grass achieving footholds in the many niches along the parapet. But contrary to popular belief, it is well maintained and still in good condition.

T. Stephens

93 The Ouse Valley Viaduct has thirty-seven semi-circular arches, each with a span of 50ft, and is 1,475ft long. Built mostly in 1840, bricks were brought by barges up the River Ouse and the Ouse River Navigation channels. It is one of the best-known railway landmarks in Sussex and a masterpiece of Victorian engineering. A marked feature is the set of four 'temples' or 'pavilions' at each end, the northern set being featured in this view taken from the rising slopes on the south-east side, a favourite vantage point for early to mid-morning photography. Such an occasion was the southbound run of the RCTS all-Pullman special on 5th October 1952 commemorating the centenary of Brighton Works. The locomotive, Brighton Atlantic No. 32424 *Beachy Head*, recorded a top speed of 75 m.p.h. near Haywards Heath and, despite signal checks, improved on the one-hour schedule.

D.B. Clayton

94 The grandeur of the Ouse Valley Viaduct captured from the north end as, in the late afternoon light with the ridge of Borde Hill on the skyline, a Southern Counties Touring Society special returns from Eastbourne. The locomotive, rebuilt Bulleid Pacific No. 34108 *Wincanton*, was pressed into service at the last minute when the booked engine failed at Nine Elms, hence the run down condition typical of those survivors which made it into the final year of Southern steam. The end was near when this shot was taken on 19th March 1967 and indeed this is believed to be the last BR steam working ever in Sussex. When admiring the fine structure it is worth reminding oneself of the great credit due to David Mocatta, the L&B architect, and John Rastrick, its builder, in bridging the broad valley of the modest Ouse river at heights varying from forty feet at the ends to ninety-six feet at the centre, the river below providing the main means of access for the eleven million bricks used in the construction. Incredibly the contract price, including approaches and the pleasant stone ornamentation, amounted to just £38,500!   *J.G. Mallinson*

95 In the pleasant winter light, N Class 2-6-0 No. 31410 of Stewarts Lane is photographed south of Balcombe in charge of a Christmas mail train. The line passes through shallow cuttings making a generous curve to keep well clear of the grounds of Balcombe Place on the east side, and leads up towards the heights of Balcombe Forest.   *G. Siviour*

96 North of Balcombe Tunnel the double track main line opens up to four tracks, the stretch from Earlswood through to beyond Three Bridges being viewed as a racing ground for express trains. 'West Country' Class No. 34047 *Callington* speeds southwards with the 11.40 a.m. Birmingham (New Street) – Hastings on 8th August 1953. Five years later the Bulleid Pacific was rebuilt with air-smoothed casing removed. The setting is the northern part of Balcombe Forest, forming part of the larger complex of St. Leonards Forest, which reaches out westwards through Handcross to Horsham. Today the M23 crosses at this particular point and the scene only remains in photographs such as this.   *S.C. Nash*

97 The locomotive portrayed is of particular interest. It is H1 Class No. 2039 *Hartland Point* which in 1947 was experimentally modified by Bulleid at Brighton Works prior to the introduction of his 'Leader' class. It was fitted with sleeve valve gear, new cylinders, outside steampipes, a multiple jet blastpipe and large-diameter chimney. The Westinghouse air pump is prominent at the side of the smokebox. This 'guinea pig' only worked public passenger services for a very short time before being scrapped in 1951. Note the absence of headcode discs, possibly indicating a trial working. This picture shows part of the twenty-seven arch London Road viaduct built in 1845/6, while the lengthy roof of Lover's Walk electric multiple unit inspection shed is just visible. At one time there were carriage sidings on the north side of the line at this point – hence the area of level ground.   *Lens of Sutton*

THE EAST COAST LINE

98 This portrait, taken in the late afternoon light, shows the distant Brighton conurbation skyline of chapels and terraced housing blended into a uniform shadowy haze. But sharply in focus is E5 Class No. 2592, built at Brighton Works in 1904 to the design of Robert Billinton and surviving until 1953. The attractive station is London Road, opened on 1st October 1877, with staggered platforms and a stately classical-lined two storey building on the south side housing the main station offices and apartments   ⁿly visible behind the telegraph pole on the left. The platforms are linked by a subway, the footbridge simply carrying a public r... across the site. The sidings seen at the rear of the 'Birdcage' set have long since gone. The absence of conductor rails and . locomotive's full Southern number dates the photograph to between 1931 and the 1935 electrification.   *O.J. Morris*

99 A stirring sight at Kemp Town Junction where the branch led round to Lewes Road Station and, by viaduct and tunnel, to the Kemp ~~Town~~ terminus. The 12.5 p.m. Brighton–Tonbridge accelerates past the signal box in the capable charge of L Class 4-4-0 ~~No.~~ ̴ ̴ ̴ ̴ 3 of Tonbridge shed. The five-coach stopping train consists of a pair of former LB&SCR coaches and an *ex*-works 'Birdcage' ~~brake. Th~~e date is 12th March 1955. On the right is the Brighton abattoir which was served by a siding. The train has just passed through Ditchling Road Tunnel (sixty-six yards) and is emerging from the short cutting at whose exit Kemp Town Junction was sited.

J.J. Smith

100 The 8.3 a.m. London Bridge–Brighton via Sheffield Park train makes a leisurely ascent of Falmer bank on 7th August 1950, in keeping with its journey time of over two hours to make it to the coast. It was the eastern approach to Falmer Tunnel that was the really steep climb involving just over three miles of 1 in 88. The location is near Ashcombe House, two miles out of Lewes, the trail of smoke paralleling the A27 road just visible, and behind it new housing development over Houndean Bottom as Lewes perceptibly swallows up the downland tracts. The locomotive is a veteran Wainwright E Class No. 31275, a Bricklayers Arms resident, in its penultimate year of operation. The mid-1930s Maunsell corridor coaches at least provided some consolation for the long-suffering passengers who patronised this secondary route to Brighton.

J.J. Smith

101 Conversation piece at Lewes, as the driver of Marsh Atlantic tank No. 2083 exchanges a few words with a member of the station staff. The Brighton side boasted four roads, the furthest track adjoining the main station area having a platform face on both sides (since filled in). But in those seemingly sunny Southern days the station scene is full of interest, the quaint yet attractive bridge linking the platforms, the supporting ironwork, station seating and large poster advertising Brighton Races, whose picture makes up for the distinct lack of scenery at this end of the station. A peep over the roof of the train reveals the rising slopes of Malling Hill. The picture was taken in the late 1940s which accords with the locomotive's number and the wartime all-black livery, but the 'target' station name signs must be in their prime. *R.A. Lissenden Collection*

102 The townscape of Lewes forms the backcloth to this pre-1935 electrification photograph. The county town of East Sussex, Lewes was built on a hill overlooking the River Ouse and crowned with a vital fortress that commanded the gap in the downs. This is seen towering above the tiers of elderly generations of housing facing on to Lansdowne Place. Behind the white fence ran the goods avoiding lines; in front of the gate is part of the dock platform for unloading cattle and horses. D Class tank locomotive No. 2283 stands in the down loop platform and, as its headcode indicates, is bound for Seaford; the date *circa* 1933. *Lens of Sutton*

103 Photographs of WD 'Austerity' 2-8-0s working on the Southern are uncommon. The class was built for the Ministry of Supply during World War II, and many saw service abroad before returning to Great Britain following the end of hostilities. About fifty members of the class were nominally allocated to the Southern Region out of a total of more than 700. Many were stored out of use at centres like Longmoor, awaiting overhaul following war service, and never actually worked before being transferred away to other regions. No. 90234 (formerly WD No. 77321) of Bricklayers Arms is seen on 1st July 1950 with an up goods from Eastbourne coming off the main electrified line in the foreground and heading into Lewes East sidings. The shallow line of the downs behind the train marks Beddingham Hill. To the left lies the works of the Lewes Portland Cement Co., Eastwoods from 1929, which closed in 1981. The site is now occupied by a light industrial estate. Slightly forward from it and not immediately visible the River Ouse flows past between dyked banks.
S.C. Nash

104 Any mention of steam in the Sussex landscape must surely conjure up a picture of a train crossing the River Ouse in front of the panoramic shelf of the chalk downs at Southerham. On 17th July 1934, one of Lawson Billinton's elegant L Class 4-6-4T locomotives, No. 2330, takes a Victoria–Eastbourne express across Southerham Bridge. First in the formation comes a 'Birdcage' 3-set, then a pair of Pullmans, concluding with four Maunsell coaches. The industrialised eastern outskirts of Lewes at Cliffe and South Malling are clearly defined, with the villas of the well-to-do encroaching upon the western slopes of Malling Down. Rewarding of interest is the detail of the bridge, river and towpath. Note the materials left by the trackside, the whole corner in the foreground being something of a builder's shanty.   *Lens of Sutton*

105 The scene at Southerham (named after a nearby farm) late in King Edward VII's reign. In February 1909 E4 Class No. 466 not only lost its former name *Honor Oak* but underwent a rebuild acquiring a Marsh I2 class boiler and, among other additions, a smokebox door of the protruding 'dished' variety. It served much of its later life at the Southern's new Norwood shed from which it was withdrawn at the end of 1958. Though the signal is 'off' for Polegate, No. 466 has come to a stop, the driver seizing the opportunity to exchange words with a passing ganger who is standing in front of one of Corrall's coal wagons. The variety of wagons, mostly loaded with coal, would provide any modeller of the period with valuable evidence; the three cattle trucks are heavily limecoated, a prevalent practice at this time, and are standing at the point where the railway crosses the Ouse.

M.P. Bennett/Bluebell Archives

106 Landscape submerged! During early November 1960 the Lewes area was affected by severe flooding, the first consequence of which was the cancellation of services to London when water rose above the conductor rails of platforms 1 to 3 at Lewes Station on Thursday 3rd November. Later that day the remaining area of the station was engulfed by rising flood water and it was completely closed to electric trains. Services from Brighton to Eastbourne were maintained by steam traction using spare coaching stock normally used on the Uckfield line, where services had been abandoned. Steam-hauled trains were supplemented by two 6-car Hastings line diesel units. Motive power employed ranged from K, N and U class Moguls to BR Standard class 4 2-6-4Ts and 4-6-0s. These arrangements lasted for almost four days until mid-morning on Sunday 6th November when electric services were restored. Lewes bonfire celebrations that year must have been the soggiest ever! In this photograph K Class 2-6-0 No. 32341 is seen near Beddingham Crossing hauling the 9.12 a.m. Brighton to Eastbourne train on 5th November. The tidal Glynde Reach, which would normally have been visible at this point, is virtually lost beneath the artificial lake which covers the adjoining fields. Two extraordinary occurrences during the flood emergency were the appearance of a former LB&SCR 'Terrier' 0-6-0T which made a sortie down the Seaford branch hauling a single passenger coach, and the remarkable sight of a resourceful Lewes signalman rowing out to his post on the Friday morning.

S.C. Nash

107 Approaching Glynde in the watery afternoon sunshine of Guy Fawkes Day 1960 is N Class 2-6-0 No. 31825 of Bricklayers Arms shed with the 1.44 p.m. Brighton to Eastbourne train. The shoulder of Mount Caburn rises on the right, while the even downlands in the left distance loom behind Rodmell. The buffer stops behind the last coach of the Maunsell 4-set mark the start of the long siding which formerly fed an extensive goods yard on either side of Glynde Station. At the turn of the century there were at least five different branch sidings fanning out to nearby clay pits and chalk quarries, and one of the latter, the Balcombe Pit, could boast of two narrow gauge systems feeding into the standard gauge connections.   *S.C. Nash*

108 A midsummer pastorale at Glynde displaying a fairly luxuriant growth of trees and bushes in this somewhat sheltered gap between the downs. Dominating the landscape is Mount Caburn, almost 500 feet above sea level. Behind the train a herd of cows wander reluctantly up to the side of the road bridge. The road runs through the trees and off the picture to the right to Glyndebourne which lies beneath the protected eastern slopes of Mount Caburn, not suffering exposure from the prevalent Channel winds from the south-west. Gleaming Gresley coaches comprise a Loughton (Essex) to Eastbourne excursion on 21st June 1959 behind U1 Class 2-6-0 No. 31892 of Stewarts Lane shed.   *S.C. Nash*

109 L&NER stock again, with another excursion from east London. The four leading vehicles are in the post-nationalisation 'plum and spilt milk' livery, and the third and fourth coaches appear to be articulated. In the midsummer evening light the 7.3 p.m. return excursion from Eastbourne to Gidea Park passes through the shallow cutting near Folkington, a mile west out of Polegate, on 29th June 1952. The locomotive is a Maunsell L1 No. 31787, which will hand over its train at New Cross Gate to an ER locomotive and then coast down the spur line to its home depot of Bricklayers Arms for cleaning and disposal. *J.J. Smith*

110 The Pevensey Levels covered a vast area of low lying land trapped behind the shingle of Pevensey Bay, stretching from the northern outskirts of Eastbourne to Cooden Reach and as far north as Herstmonceux. Each little segment of levels was known by a separate name, e.g. Horse Eye Level to the east of Hailsham. The background to this picture illustrates Willingdon Level in Edwardian days. E4 Class No. 469, which in Robert Billinton's time bore the proud name of *Beachy Head* (later revived on No. 2424, the last Marsh Atlantic to survive), trundles a short train of loaded coal wagons, destined for either the locomotive depot or for domestic use in Eastbourne, down the west side of the Stone Cross triangle between Polegate and Hampden Park.

M.P. Bennett/Bluebell Archives

111 The built-up skyline of Eastbourne makes the setting for the late afternoon departure of the Birkenhead through train on its last leg round Pevensey Bay to Hastings on 15th September 1955. L Class 4-4-0 No. 31764 of St. Leonards shed heads two Maunsell 3-sets in differing liveries. The electric unit on the right is a Southern Railway 6-car Pantry unit introduced in connection with the electrification to Eastbourne in 1935. On the far right stands the signal box which is still in use at the time of writing.   *P.J. Lynch*

112 The Crumbles line takes its name from the massive ¾-mile wide shingle bank which forms the coastline between Eastbourne and Pevensey. The material was used by the LB&SCR for track ballasting, and in 1862 a private agreement was signed with the landowner, the Duke of Devonshire, whereby the Company undertook to purchase not less than 48,000 cubic yards of shingle a year. The single line curved away just over half a mile north of Eastbourne Station and round to the east for a further 1¼ miles, crossing the Langney Turnpike, today's A259, on the level before heading out towards Langney Point and the now legendary 'Ballast Hole'. There were other offshoots, the chief one being to the works of the Eastbourne Gas Company opened under a similar agreement in 1870, and it is on this stretch that C2X Class No. 2528 of Brighton shed is seen propelling the midday train through the allotments to the gas works on 3rd October 1948.   *J.J. Smith*

113 The Crumbles line in its middle section near Roselands left the built-up area of Eastbourne's extended suburbs and curved round its fringe over a flat expanse intersected by numerous drainage channels, whose time-weakened structures required a 5 m.p.h. speed restriction. This unfenced stretch, with a next to empty background, was used by the LB&SCR for its official photographs, both individual locomotives and even a complete train like the 'Southern Belle' Pullman. E4 Class No. 32518 is passing this location propelling its train on 28th October 1950. Motive power over the years included classes E1 through to the occasional E5, while C2Xs were also often in evidence. The line finally succumbed on 30th April 1960, but odd lengths of rail set in concrete and decaying sleepers were still to be seen along its course in recent years.
                    J.J. Smith

114 Eastbourne Gas Works was built in the early 1870s and was served by a branch siding from the Crumbles line. It closed in 1967. Here two of its stalwarts, displaying the ownership of the South Eastern Gas Board, seem unaware of their impending doom on a sunny afternoon in April 1964. Both are Avonside 0-4-0STs, *Anne* was built in 1914, *Mary* five years earlier, and were originally based at Sydenham Gas Works, being finally broken up in 1968. The siting of the painted name below the worksplate on the cabside is unusual. The works in its heyday consumed some 40,000 tons of coal a year, but most of this returned to rail haulage in the form of coke. *S.C. Nash*

115 Eastbourne's first main shed replaced an earlier one in 1876, and stood within sight of the terminus. Cramped conditions in the semi-roundhouse and expanding services led to the construction of a new depot in 1911/2, probably the LB&SCR's finest shed, spacious and well laid out on a virgin site on the flat Willingdon Levels adjacent to the line on its west side. Built with seven through roads, reductions in the establishment of locomotives following the 1935 electrification led to it becoming something of a white elephant, and a host of veteran LB&SCR pre-grouping locomotives ripe for withdrawal were kept in store for the duration of the war, mostly D class tanks and B4s. The shed never recovered from extensive bomb damage, and remained in an increasing state of dereliction until the end of steam. The scene at the side of the shed on 25th October 1959 shows a rare visitor, E1R Class No. 32697, standing out of steam. A Maunsell rebuild of a Stroudley E1, the new class was designed for service on the lightly-laid North Devon and Cornwall Junction line opened between Torrington and Halwill in 1925, the trailing pair of wheels helping to spread the weightload. This was possibly the only time one of this class visited Eastbourne, having been based for banking duties at Exmouth Junction and *en route* for Ashford, where it was broken up the following month. The Eastbourne shedmaster, either hard pressed for good engines or just simply sympathetic, put the ill-fated guest to work on carriage and yard piloting before sending it eastwards on 22nd November. To the right beyond the electrified running lines there is a glimpse of railwaymen's allotments breaking up the flat landscape. *J.J. Smith*

116 The 6.40 p.m. Eastbourne–Polegate goods passes the junction of the lines giving access to Eastbourne shed on 19th July 1951. The train engine, I1X Class No. 2002 still in Southern livery, would go on to work the 7.10 p.m. van train from Polegate to Lewes while the pilot, C2X Class No. 32438 of Brighton shed, took the goods from Polegate yard to Lewes East sidings, and later to Brighton Top Yard. This could have been No. 2002's last working, as its recorded date of withdrawal is July 1951! The Crumbles line is on the left hidden by bushes, and the allotment area on view has now been built upon with small factories and houses. *J.J. Smith*

117 Q1 Class No. 33037 of Tonbridge shed takes the 5.49 p.m. Eastbourne to Hastings (12.35 p.m. *ex*-Leicester, hence the London Midland Region stock) over the Willingdon Loop spur line near Willingdon Junction on 30th July 1960. The spotless condition of the locomotive, rare for this goods class, suggests a recent visit to the shops at Ashford. Between the stunted tree and the train the flat outline of the stretch of downs between Coombe Hill and Pea Down behind Willingdon can just be discerned. *J.J. Smith*

118 Eastbourne had been reached as a branch from Polegate off the 1846 line to Bulverhythe on the outskirts of Hastings. To obviate reversal at Polegate by Eastbourne to Hastings trains, the Willingdon Loop (*see* previous photograph) was laid in 1871, rejoining the direct line at Stone Cross Junction, twenty chains west of Pevensey. Stone Cross derives its name from a local cross-roads on the A27 a quarter of a mile north of the junction. The photographer is standing outside the northern section of the triangle looking across it towards the South Downs behind Willingdon on 15th August 1959, as K Class No. 32350 speeds eastwards with the 8.43 a.m. special empty working between Polegate and Hastings, comprising Maunsell 9-set No. 218. Closed in 1969, the line was lifted in part leaving a siding for some years. Today all trains along the coast must reverse at Eastbourne.
J.J. Smith

119 This fascinating view shows a westbound train passing the construction site of St. Leonards diesel depot which was built to maintain the distinctive narrow-bodied diesel units employed on the Charing Cross–Hastings route. Inspection pits and foundations are clearly visible. The depot closed for maintenance purposes in 1986, but the buildings remain at the time of writing, stabling electric units plus a few diesel units employed on the Hastings–Ashford line. It was close by here that the original 1846 Bulverhythe terminus for Hastings was sited. The line runs very close to the sea at only two points, at Cooden Reach and here, within sight of the built-up hilly sandstone ridges of Hastings. The train is the 10.51 a.m. Hastings to Leicester pictured on 1st September 1956 with London Midland Region stock and N Class locomotive No. 31874, the only member of this once numerous class to survive into preservation, on the Mid-Hants Railway.
D.T. Rowe

120 The exquisite lines of a Wainwright-designed L class 4-4-0 are seen to perfection as No. 31767 passes its home shed of St. Leonards, outside which some vintage SE&CR veterans are standing, including E Class No. 31587. The depot is hidden by the train, the 12.30 p.m. Hastings to Manchester, which has just passed St. Leonards West Marina Station on 21st July 1951. The sidings on the right curving away form part of a medium-sized yard, whose goods shed just appears at the edge of the picture. In the background stands the ridge – well patronised by developers – above Bopeep Tunnel, through which the railway burrows to arrive at St. Leonards (Warrior Square) Station.   *J.J. Smith*

121 St. Leonards West Marina seen from the east on 7th April 1958. The shed occupies a cramped location, having made demanding inroads into the adjacent hillside. All the locomotive servicing facilities are visible; the shed building was reconstructed in 1949. The LB&SCR cottages up on the hill were not in the best of positions for obtaining clean washing on a Monday morning! A local electric train comprising two 2-NOL units makes a stop at West Marina Station. The locomotives in the picture are, from left to right: 'Terrier' No. 32678, since preserved at Minehead and now at the Kent and East Sussex Railway, on coal stage duty; D1 Class 4-4-0 No. 31246, turned for its return working to Ashford; N Class 2-6-0 No. 31851 of Bricklayers Arms; and fellow shedmate 'Schools' Class No. 30934 *St. Lawrence*, turned round for working back to London.
    D.W. Winkworth

122 L Class No. 1768 runs into Hastings on a working from Tonbridge in July 1939. In the background is the distinguished looking Linton Road bridge whose architect faced problems over the need for differing widths for the various spans. Behind the train can be seen the eastern portal of the 788 yards-long Hastings Tunnel. The couple of vintage cars seen on the right would fetch a handsome price today!
    J.P. Wilson

123 Just over a mile south-east of Plumpton in the flat countryside to the north of the downs, watered by the River Ouse and its many tributaries, lies the pretty village of East Chiltington. Here 'Schools' Class No. 30922 *Marlborough*, a Stewarts Lane engine, hastens the 3.24 p.m. Newhaven boat train on its way to Victoria on 4th April 1953.   *J.J. Smith*

HAYWARDS HEATH TO SEAFORD

124 A classic portrait, by E.J. Bedford of Lewes, of a Victoria–Newhaven boat train speeding through the idyllic setting of Cooksbridge Station in the late 1880s. The impressively shining Stroudley locomotive is his pioneer Single No. 326 *Grosvenor*, with Driver Schofield on the footplate, hauling the 'Down Continental', duly bearing a 'double diamond' disc. Bedford stated that the train was travelling at 60 m.p.h., emphasising to his credit the difficulty of taking successful photographs of moving objects at this early date. This relatively flat district was well provided with trees which hem in the platform on the left, while the setting of the goods yard and sheds is rewarding of detailed study. Chatfields, the timber merchants whose premises are visible on the right, continue to run their business from the same site today.   *E.J. Bedford/Bluebell Archives*

125 Approaching Cooksbridge from the south-east is Stroudley 'Gladstone' 0-4-2 No. 199 (formerly *Samuel Laing*), built in 1888 and based for almost all its working life at Brighton. It is seen here having received a Marsh chimney and tall dome, but retaining its Stroudley boiler with its spring balance safety valves leaving it looking somewhat disjointed. This pre-1914 photograph taken in overcast conditions, which blur the outline of the mist-ridden downs and the cutting from which the train has emerged, nevertheless exudes power as No. 199 makes speed on its way towards London. *Lens of Sutton*

126 The same scene nearly half a century later – spot the changes: live rails, more modern signalling, lineside fencing replacing hedgerows, but little else. The setting, the approach to the level crossing at Cooksbridge, shows the line emerging from a deep cutting as it carves through an outlying ridge of downland chalk to achieve a more direct entry to Lewes than that detouring towards Barcombe and the flats of the River Ouse. On 21st August 1955, Class 4MT 2-6-4T No. 42104, built and then based at Brighton to supplement the declining ranks of the Marsh Atlantic tanks withdrawn in the immediate post-nationalisation years, hauls the 1.0 p.m. special goods *ex*-Newhaven consisting of twenty-eight wagons and a brake van. *J.J. Smith*

127 Lewes was the subject of several realignments, one particular major rebuilding being completed in 1889. 17th June saw the first services using the new station. E.J. Bedford, who lived at Lewes during this period, was there to photograph the first down working which he describes as a newspaper train hauled by a G class Stroudley Single. There was quite a crowd witnessing the scene from the roadbridge overlooking the North signal box, in addition to the construction staff still busy putting the finishing touches to the new station which has as its backcloth a sylvan screen hiding the historic town, though the topmost point of Lewes Castle can be seen on the skyline directly above the locomotive's chimney.

E.J. Bedford/F. Burtt Collection NRM

128 Former LB&SCR Atlantic No. 2423 *The Needles*, in charge of a southbound boat train for Newhaven Harbour, has taken the points at Southerham Junction to veer away from the line to Eastbourne on the right. The picture was taken prior to electrification which was completed on 7th July 1935. The train consists entirely of Maunsell stock, apart from the Pullman Car. In the distance lies the chalk cutting leading to the junction protected by a nice selection of tall LB&SCR lower-quadrant signals. The Marsh Atlantics were associated with the Newhaven boat traffic, particularly following their displacement from the Brighton main line by electrification.

Lens of Sutton

129 Nearing Southerham Junction from the opposite direction is an up relief excursion train hauled by a Stroudley G class Single whose sanding jets are working furiously. The train consists of a Stroudley luggage van followed by a Billinton close-coupled suburban block set, built at the turn of the century. The billowing trail of smoke hangs long in the dank atmosphere screening the heights of the South Downs at Beddingham Hill, while a glimpse past the front of the locomotive reveals part of the narrow gap between the downland ridges created by Glynde Reach, through which the line to Eastbourne and Hastings squeezed a reasonably level passage.

E.J. Bedford/Bluebell Archives

130 The same scene some sixty years later on a much clearer day, with the treeless line of the downs forming a graceful backcloth, marred only by the white gash on the far right, the result of decades of working at Rodmell Cement Works. On 13th July 1963 Maunsell N Class Moguls Nos. 31864 and 31869 head for Southerham Junction in the soft evening light with the 7.0 p.m. Newhaven Harbour to Newcastle-upon-Tyne, comprising eighteen bogies – three coaches and fifteen vans – the latter accommodating empty pigeon baskets returning north.

J.J. Smith

131 At the point of the curve seen in the distance in the previous photograph, two miles south of Southerham Junction, the line crosses Glynde Reach by means of a shallow girder bridge supported by strengthened timber baulks. This tributary of the River Ouse at one time carried commercial traffic, mostly chalk from quarries at Glynde which is two miles distant upstream. In front of the locomotive to the left is the other shoulder of the downs leading up to Mount Caburn, which rises to almost 500 feet above sea level. The rebuilt 'Battle of Britain' Class Pacific is No. 34089 *602 Squadron*, seen heading tender-first from Brighton to pick up a working from Newhaven Harbour on 10th June 1962.

J.J. Smith

132 The traditional setting for a Newhaven boat train, complete with Marsh Atlantic at the head! The 4.52 p.m. Sunday service delivering cross-Channel passengers on the final part of their journey to Victoria leaves behind the port of Newhaven in the distance and sets out across the marshy flood plain of the tidal River Ouse. The locomotive is No. 32426 *St. Albans Head* and the formation includes a pair of the customary luggage vans and the Pullman Car *Myrtle* in the line of a dozen passenger coaches, with four Maunsell carriages in green and seven Bulleid vehicles in red and cream livery. The location is milepost 55 measured from London; the signal box in the distance is Newhaven North Box, put in during the first world war to control expanded siding facilities, and at this stage of its history known as 'A' Box. The date is 12th August 1951.

J.J. Smith

133 The Newhaven West Harbour Tramway was planned under an Act of 1863 to serve the wharves and other buildings on the west side of the harbour at the mouth of the River Ouse. The plan involved taking the line across the river on a swing bridge and was part of a general scheme of improvement works by the Harbour Trustees. The LB&SCR's undertaking to construct the tramway was not immediately implemented, though the swing bridge was ready at the end of 1866. The approach to the bridge from the west side is on a sharp curve on which a 'Terrier', the only class of engine allowed on the lightly-laid track, No. 32678, stands at the exit of the Engineer's Yard siding. The west side of the town spreading up over the chalk ridges forms the backdrop. The disused wooden lighthouse with its weathervane adds to the flavour of antiquity in this little corner of the town. The date is 27th July 1963, very near the end for No. 32678 as its last trip was on 10th August that year. The whole of this delightful foreground setting has been obliterated by the construction in 1972 of a ring-road through the town. *J.J. Smith*

134 The branch to Newhaven opened to passengers on 8th December 1847 with high hopes of what was confidently expected to become a great port, the 'Liverpool of the South', according to a guide book of 1852. The packet service remained tidal, a report describing the harbour of Newhaven as 'a mere creek with only two or three feet on the bar at low water'. So it was no wonder that the Newhaven Harbour Company was created in 1878 under LB&SCR auspices. Moles were built, together with a quay for packets and a harbour station alongside. Fixed sailings commenced at the start of April 1889 and continue to this day. The harbour scene on 5th May 1960 is captured complete with dredger, while the downs ride away on the horizon. The ferry to Dieppe is the *Londres*, moored opposite the customs sheds and warehouses with groups of BR wagons and vans visible on the quay. The 'Terrier' in the foreground standing on the West Quay is the former Brighton Works shunter No. 32635 in Stroudley's gamboge yellow livery, filling in for the regular engine called away for boiler washout and servicing at Brighton. *W.M.J. Jackson*

135 Near the harbour entrance, close to the Hope Inn, the West Harbour tramway curved round the chalk headland in a westerly direction. Just short of the breakwater there was a siding but no run round loop. This served the Harbourmaster's storeshed for his building materials, and from here boulders, shingle and chalk ballast were taken up the line. All wagons were fly shunted, and those on view include several former LB&SCR examples. The 'Terrier', No. 2636, was still known by its former name *Fenchurch*, having been very much part of the Newhaven scene since 1898 when it was sold to the Newhaven Harbour Co. for £500. It retained Stroudley livery until 1902, and its name until 1917. In 1921 the inscription 'Newhaven Harbour Company' was displayed on its tank sides, and on being absorbed into the Southern Railway continued to work the harbour lines into BR days until 1955. Today the life of the 118 years-old locomotive continues on the Bluebell Railway. Some clue to the date is given through the fact that No. 2636 is here carrying a set of LB&SCR gilt numerals discovered at Brighton Works in 1935, and was one of the fortunate few to have them so applied.
C.C.B. Herbert/NRM

136 'Terrier' No. 32635, formerly Brighton Works shunter DS 377, propels a group of wagons on to the neck of the breakwater, possibly for photographic purposes, for the final few hundred yards of the line saw little use at this late date in its history, May 1960. The arrival of the Stroudley liveried 'Terrier' was a rare photographic opportunity, for Brighton shed was liable to supply any of its small group of 'Terriers' as a replacement when a fellow member of the class departed to home base for attention. This location was the closest a Sussex railway line got to the sea and indeed continued a further quarter mile out into the Channel along the length of the Newhaven mole!
W.M.J. Jackson

137 On 7th October 1962, the Railway Correspondence and Travel Society ran an enthusiasts special which visited the Seaford branch, opened on 1st June 1864. Originally single, it was doubled in 1905 when Seaford station was re-built, but is now single again. The line was electrified on 7th July 1935. The special is seen passing Bishopstone Reach in mid-afternoon. Bishopstone, the only intermediate station, was said to produce the least revenue of any Sussex station until replaced by modern platforms and buildings half a mile to the south-east in 1938. The locomotives are a pair of former LB&SCR veterans, A1X Class No. 32636 and the last E6 in service, No. 32418. The E6, unlike its more fortunate companion which was later preserved, went to the scrap-heap at the end of the year. The coastal pastures of the estuary flats, close to the site of the former Tide Mills, provide good grazing for cattle.
J.J. Smith

138   The open curve approaching Culver Junction, to join the Uckfield line for the last couple of miles into Lewes, lends itself to a fine summertime portrait. The scene is right at the southern end of the East Grinstead to Lewes line which has descended along with the River Ouse to the rural flatlands of that river's flood plain. Though the locomotive carries the initial short-lived British Railways livery, this could just as well be a timeless Southern picture typical of the previous quarter-century, with its 'Birdcage' set and Maunsell coach tacked on at the back. E class 4-4-0s ran services over the line from just before the grouping, and No. s1491, based at Bricklayers Arms, heads the 4.18 p.m. London Bridge–Brighton on 4th August 1951. All except three of the unrebuilt members of the class were withdrawn that same year, No. s1491 continuing till 1953.   *J.J. Smith*

LEWES TO EAST GRINSTEAD

139   Stroudley 'Gladstone' class 0-4-2s reigned in charge of the through London–Brighton via East Grinstead services during the Edwardian period, having been relegated to secondary line duties by the new express engines designed by Robert Billinton and Earle Marsh. No. 178 (formerly *Leatherhead*) is seen standing at Barcombe's single platform on the late morning through train from Victoria to Brighton. This resplendent-looking locomotive was scrapped not long after, in 1912. At first the station was named Barcombe Cross and, being situated at the top of Barcombe High Street, proved the busiest of any between East Grinstead and Lewes. Single line it remained, though a goods loop was laid in 1905. It never reopened after the 1955 closure, not being one of the four intermediate stations mentioned in the 1877 Parliamentary Act, the relevance of which is explained in the caption to plate No. 141.   *Lens of Sutton*

140 A fulfilment of a railway photographer's wildest dreams, not the usual snap of a train passing through Cinder Hill Tunnel, but of a tunnel gantry train on Sunday 24th April 1955, with the engineering gang at work on the interior from the detached gantry wagon. The crew of C2X Class 0-6-0 No. 32440, of Brighton shed, relax in the sunshine while the others work hard in the shade! The sixty-one yards-long tunnel lay just over 300 yards south of Newick and Chailey Station, with no pretensions to a castellated portal. But it had its moment of glory during the second world war when it proved just long enough for a push-pull train to reach its shelter from machine gun attack by a German aircraft. *J.J. Smith*

141 Between 7th August 1956 and 15th March 1958 an extraordinary scenario was played out on the Lewes–East Grinstead line. This section reopened after fourteen months of a closure which was proved illegal by a local resident, Miss R.E.M. Bessemer of Chailey, who found that under the original Act of 1877 this could only be effected by Parliamentary authority and not by independent action of the railway company. BR responded with a token service of four trains a day each way which ran out of step with most connecting services at both ends, nor were through booking facilities available beyond Lewes or East Grinstead from the remaining four intermediate stations (Kingscote and Barcombe, not specified in the Act, remaining closed). The resultant poorly patronised service is seen here typified by a locomotive and single coach, both vintage LB&SCR. C2X Class No. 32536 of Three Bridges is climbing the 1 in 75 Freshfield bank with the 1.30 p.m. Lewes–East Grinstead on 27th October 1956. It is still possible to photograph steam at this rural location, now part of the Bluebell Railway. *J.J. Smith*

142   Snowscape at Horsted Keynes, with E5 Class 0-6-2T No. 2592 making a crisp start with a local bound for East Grinstead. The length of electrified rail protruding from behind the locomotive indicates a post-July 1935 date. At this period the fortunes of the class were already on the wane, being used for night-time goods workings from London to Redhill and East Grinstead and filling in the rest of the day with passenger workings out of East Grinstead. Withdrawal commenced in 1936 and only the outbreak of war saved the rest of the class from an early demise, this representative succumbing as late as 1953.   *Courtesy Brighton Library*

143   This stationscape of Horsted Keynes on 25th May 1955 conveys a far clearer impression of its salient features and blissful setting in the heart of the countryside. The tall up starter, for so long a landmark, enabled train crews to sight the arms above the station canopies at a comfortable distance ahead; it survived till the late 1960s. Another landmark to go was the pump-house water tank just discernible amongst the trees to the right of the signal box, but most of the other features remain today with additions by the Bluebell Railway of buildings and relaid sidings full of preserved rolling stock. The slopes on the late afternoon's hazy horizon of Lindfield Wood screen the line of the South Downs. The Pullman Car *Savona* at rear is *en route* from Preston Park shops to Stewarts Lane. Many odd vehicles were sent on this train, the 5.18 p.m. from Brighton, including loaded horse boxes going to destinations on the LMR and ER. If onward movement of a horse box to Willesden was required at Victoria, it would normally go forward on the 7.45 p.m. Victoria–Willesden parcels train which left from the Eastern side. As the Brighton train was not due into Victoria until 7.49 p.m., the 'connection' had to be held specially for the horse! The T9 Class 4-4-0 No. 30718 working this service was most unusual, being diagrammed specially to get the locomotive (which was *ex*-works) to its home depot at Nine Elms. The connecting electric service to Haywards Heath and Seaford is just visible behind the signal box.   *J.J. Smith*

144 The 3.28 p.m. Haywards Heath to London Bridge via East Grinstead provided the opportunity for a run behind steam at a leisurely pace all the way to London. K class Moguls were regular performers in the post-war years through to the first closure. No. 32339 of Brighton shed is seen on 14th May 1955, exactly a fortnight before this service was suspended during a rail strike, and never revived. The location is just north of Horsted Keynes near milepost 11¾ on a section of the line recently reopened by the Bluebell Railway, as the line heads into the slopes leading up to the Sharpthorne ridge. It is possible that at some distant future date the Bluebell could repair and return to service a 'Birdcage' 3-set; it already has six Bulleid coaches in use but the type of locomotive cannot be repeated. Although a representative from this class was on the Bluebell Railway Preservation Society's shortlist, the whole class was withdrawn at the end of 1962 and all were subsequently broken-up.   *J.J. Smith*

145 BR Standard Class 4 2-6-4T No. 80031 heads into Sussex in 1962 with a well-loaded train from London which will divide into Brighton and Eastbourne sections at Eridge. The train is approaching St. Margaret's Junction where the signal indicates it will take the spur line round to reach East Grinstead High Level platforms. Despite the distant signal's horizontal warning arm the driver, aware of the brief stiff climb ahead, has not shut off steam. The line of trees on the horizon behind the rear coaches lies in Surrey, for the county border is only a short distance away.   *G. Siviour*

146 The timeless branch connection scenario, with E4 Class No. 2520 being given a final shovelful of coal before departure from Three Bridges. The train, formed of an *ex-SE&CR* 'Birdcage' 3-set, stands under the overall roof of the East Grinstead bay platform in the immediate post-war period, the locomotive painted black but in 'sunshine' lettering. The buildings on this side of the station in part date back to the earliest days of the Brighton line, and the chimneys of Mocatta's original station house can be seen behind the goods wagon. Sadly the area on the eastern side of the main line, where East Grinstead and Tunbridge Wells trains used to start, was demolished in the mid-1980s, and is now occupied by a warehouse and BR's new (1985) signal box which is officially known as 'Three Bridges Area Signalling Centre'. *Lens of Sutton*

THREE BRIDGES TO TUNBRIDGE WELLS

147 In the heart of Worth Forest the line burrows through the cutting at Worth itself in a virtual arcade of trees not normally permitted to encroach and overhang the track so closely. On 19th May 1963 H Class 0-4-4T No. 31518 climbs the grade at this point with the 11.8 a.m. Three Bridges to East Grinstead, comprising a pair of Maunsell coaches converted to push-pull working. The locomotive is one of the final surviving batch of its class, allocated for these workings first at Tunbridge Wells and, in the final months, at Three Bridges shed from which the last three were all withdrawn in one fell swoop in January 1964. Another of the final trio was No. 31263, which today survives on the Bluebell Railway at Sheffield Park. *S.C. Nash*

148   Rowfant started out in 1855 as almost a private station for the local landowner, Curtis Miranda Lampson who, as part of the deal for making available the land through which the railway ran, had a very attractive and distinctive station constructed for himself, the ornamented building incorporating an alcove for his coachman to shelter from the elements. There was a brickworks on the up side approaching the station from the east, served by its own private siding. The line was single until the turn of the century when a loop, footbridge and up platform shelter were added. The footbridge was removed in later years, passengers from the East Grinstead direction having to cross by the set of boarded sleepers, over which the locomotive is passing. The carriages are astride the skew level crossing necessitated by the shallow approach angle of the local lane. The M7 class locomotive portrayed at the head of the 1.8 p.m. Three Bridges to East Grinstead train on 9th June 1963 is worthy of mention. It was withdrawn the following May, only to reappear on an enthusiasts' special in July 1964. In 1967 No. 30053 was shipped to the Steamtown Railway Museum in Vermont, U.S.A., and remained across the Atlantic until its return to this country in 1987. It was rescued by the 'Southern Repatriation Group', who have placed the L&SWR veteran on loan to the Purbeck Line at Swanage, thus returning it to one of its former haunts.   *J.J. Smith*

149   Sister M7 No. 30055, on the same 1.8 p.m. turn, pulls away from Grange Road for East Grinstead on 19th May 1963. Though the line opened in 1855, Grange Road only appeared on the railway map in 1860 in response to the developing suburbs of East Grinstead. Its single spacious platform lay adjacent to the road whose name it adopted, the level crossing controlled by the LB&SCR-style brick cabin. At this late moment in the life of the branch, the small goods yard lies deserted and overgrown in the shadow of the mature tall trees which have witnessed a century of steam through their immediate landscape. Diesel units took over the majority of workings in 1964 signalling the end of the 'foreign' pre-grouping regime of L&SWR M7s and SE&CR H class tank haulage. No. 30055 went in September 1963, and all the remaining M7s were gone by the following May.

R.A. Lissenden

150 The single line from Ashurst Junction fans out to serve the four platform faces (two islands) at East Grinstead (High Level), a 'double decker' station full of unusual interest. Behind the locomotive the spur line to the low level lines curves away. To the left of the signal, itself a splendid specimen with its mounted shunt signals nicknamed 'Tommydods' with their indicating 'hands', is a splendid view down the length of the siding alongside Longley's timber yard. Behind the train lies the High Level goods yard, originally the site of the first terminus station of 1855. The 1930s train itself is a delight with its clean D1 Class 0-4-2T and gleaming LB&SCR coaches recently ex-works. No. 2253 was to survive through the war to 1949, sister locomotive No. 32252 being the last to go in September 1950.

Lens of Sutton

151 During the early days of the Bluebell Railway a number of special trains were run by the Bluebell Railway Preservation Society. The first ran on 12th July 1959 on a circular course from Tonbridge and back via East Grinstead (where a shunt was made from the High to the Low Level), Haywards Heath, Lewes and Uckfield. The Society's efforts to organise the trip were cruelly sabotaged by a printing strike which made publicity difficult, but in the event all 280 seats on the train were taken and many prospective passengers had to be turned away. The special was hauled by a Standard 2-6-4T locomotive from Tonbridge to Tunbridge Wells West (and return) during the first and last stages of its journey, but for the lion's share of the tour Class C2X No. 32535 was in charge. It is seen here between the tunnels at the approach to East Grinstead (High Level) Station. *J.J. Smith*

152   On 13th October 1951, Brighton-built Fairburn 2-6-4T locomotive No. 42089 powers up the grade past Brambletye Crossing in charge of the 1.8 p.m. Tunbridge Wells West to London Bridge train, comprising of SE&CR 'Birdcage' and Maunsell sets of coaching stock. The section eastwards of Grinstead was mooted by the East Grinstead, Groombridge and Tunbridge Wells Railway Company. After a string of delays the line finally opened at the start of October 1866 and enjoyed custom for just over a century, closing on the first day of 1967. On the right is the crossing keeper's house which has seen considerable expansion from the original dwelling. One of its first occupants was the signalman disciplined following the Clayton Tunnel accident of 1861. He finished his days on crossing keeper's duties here at Brambletye, which lies half a mile west of Forest Row. The electricity pylon stands on the rising slopes of Ashurstwood.

J.J. Smith

153   E4 Class No. 32581 ambles the 11.30 a.m. Tunbridge Wells West to Three Bridges train along the predominantly flat countryside of the upper Medway valley which the line follows all the way to Ashurst Junction. The course of the stream flows by the hedgerow immediately behind the telegraph pole. The bridge in the distance carries the lane to a house by the name of Lower Parrock which lies between Forest Row and Hartfield. The still well-maintained 0-6-2T, based at Tunbridge Wells, blends favourably with Maunsell 4-set No. 490. The photograph was taken in the mid-1950s; No. 32581 remained in traffic until April 1962.   *Pamlin Prints*

154 Literally steam in the landscape, when K Class Mogul No. 32346 chose to descend Forest Row bank too hastily on 3rd March 1954 with a Three Bridges to Buxted engineer's train, and became derailed at the end of Forest Row's sand drag. The line was cleared that night, but the operation to recover the culprit was not undertaken until 7th March with the call up of the heavy brigade comprised of two breakdown cranes, one from Brighton and ar ner from the London area. This was not the end c' tory for on 8th April a test run was arranged by t' power department with a train of similar co ght running from Three Bridges to Gro oack. The engine was No. 32351 which made the descent of Forest Row bank, let it be said in better weather than the former occasion, without incident. Its return up the bank with a very heavy load was described by a bystander as 'something memorable to be seen and heard'. *J.J. Smith*

155 Another K class locomotive heads a weedkilling train on 3rd June 1962, timed from East Grinstead at 10.35 a.m. and *en route* for Tunbridge Wells West, past milepost 42 in Gallypot Wood, a mile west of Hartfield. The lightly wooded scenery at this spot made it a favourite location for photographers. Pictures of weedkilling trains from the steam era are uncommon: nowadays tank wagons are used in place of the line of antiquated pre-grouping tenders. No. 32349, based at Three Bridges shed, had five months steam left in her, all seventeen members of the class being taken out of traffic in November and December 1962.
J.J. Smith

156 Another view of the pioneer Bluebell Railway Preservation Society special passing the goods yard at Hartfield on its approach to the station behind C2X Class No. 32535, one of the double-domed variety of this class designed by Robert Billinton. Built in 1900 it was converted to class C2X incorporating a Marsh boiler as late as December 1939. The second dome housed Lawson Billinton's top feed arrangement. No. 32535 was a Three Bridges locomotive during the last twelve years of its working life, which ceased in February 1962. The leading coach, a BR Standard Mk. 1 in red and cream livery, was reserved for a special party of Bluebell supporters; two Maunsell 3-sets completed the formation. The wooded crest on the left is Perryhill while the ever close River Medway flows amongst the lower trees at the far end of the field. *The late Derek Cross*

LEWES TO TUNBRIDGE WELLS

157 Lewes, the county town of East Sussex, probably has the most complicated railway history of any town in the county. The first railway came in 1846: that was the Brighton to Lewes route which was opened on 8th June, but within a few weeks was extended to Bulverhythe, near Hastings. Just over a year later, on 2nd October 1847, the line from Keymer Junction was opened, and finally twenty years afterwards in 1868, the route from Tunbridge Wells. Stations have existed at various sites in Lewes, the present station being the third! In this photograph the tracks bearing right in the foreground follow the course of the original main line through the town, which was reduced to a goods avoiding line when the existing station was opened on a new alignment in 1889. A special goods working, hauled by BR Standard tank locomotive No. 80015, is heading towards Uckfield on a viaduct that also dates from the alterations carried out in connection with the opening of the 1889 station. In this photograph, besides revealing a little of the history of railways at Lewes, the train itself is of particular interest as it was one of the few to run during the ASLEF strike in 1955. The locomotive had earlier powered an Eastbourne–Lewes passenger train, prior to taking out this unscheduled goods working from Lewes to Crowborough at 4.30 p.m. on 5th June.

J.J. Smith

158 No. 31492, a Maunsell rebuild of a Wainwright D class, gathers speed away from Barcombe Mills Station on a Tonbridge–Brighton service on 27th October 1956. The station is just visible in the background, and the train is travelling along the Barcombe Levels close to the flood plain of the River Ouse, towards Culver Junction. There it will meet the line from East Grinstead which is visible on the left. The whole of the Hurst Green Junction–Lewes line was slated for closure in the Beeching Report, but local opposition saved the route north of Uckfield which remains a vital link for commuters. The section between Uckfield and Lewes succumbed to closure, however, on 23rd February 1969, the allegedly poor condition of the viaduct at Lewes being a crucial factor in the closure decision. Plans to reinstate this missing link have been mooted, but have not yet come to fruition. It will be noted that all the Tonbridge–Brighton trains depicted in this section are formed of narrow-bodied 'Restriction 1' stock to permit passage through Grove Tunnel at Tunbridge Wells.

J.H.W. Kent

159 Barcombe village was fortunate enough to have two stations offering services to London along diverse routes. Barcombe Mills Station was originally known as Barcombe. The village would have had a third station if a planned railway from Beckenham to Brighton had materialised. No. 32378 is an LB&SCR D3 Class tank locomotive, by this late date – 7th August 1950 – rare in appearance on this line, and working out its final days, probably the best locomotive that could be found for the 3.11 p.m. Tunbridge Wells West–Lewes working. Behind the down platform a siding curved round and down the road by the cottages to the former mill which lay behind the tall trees, the River Ouse only a stone's throw away.

J.J. Smith

160 The Uckfield line workings certainly seemed a repository for locomotives working out their last days. On 19th June 1951, I1X Class No. 2002 heads the 7.37 p.m. Tunbridge Wells West–Brighton in charge of 6-car Maunsell set No. 471, quite a respectable load for the old-timer judging by the burnt paint on the smokebox door. It was withdrawn the following month. The summer's evening sun graces the train as it approaches a crossing of the River Ouse south of Isfield. *J.J. Smith*

161 Just north of Isfield, N Class Mogul No. 31850 heads a south-bound working over tracks running above the flood plain of a tributary of the River Ouse, which runs through the middle background but is hidden from view. The location is half-way between Uckfield and Isfield, whose station was restored in 1983/4 and is now the base of the Lavender Line preservation centre. *G. Siviour*

162 Brighton Atlantics worked out of Victoria to Brighton via Eridge in the early to mid-1950s. This Sunday working, on 26th June 1955, the 9.7 a.m. to Brighton, restarts from its stop at Uckfield, passing the delightful signal cabin controlling the interesting three-way points in the yard in a truly rural setting. No. 32421 *South Foreland* was retired in the following May with flawed bogie frames, and laid aside until withdrawn that August. Uckfield is today a terminal station, served by diesel units which operate to and from Oxted; in the rush hour some through services to London are provided. Prior to the coming of the railway, goods traffic was transported using a cut off the Ouse canal which terminated just a couple of miles west of Uckfield at Shortbridge. *J.J. Smith*

163 A very rare shot of a breakdown crane on the move for a pre-planned job. Note the 'Birdcage' riding van which apparently has a stove-pipe chimney protruding through the roof. The locomotive, Maunsell Q Class No. 30549, is in its final year, having been based on the Central Section from 1955 including a short penultimate spell at Brighton, whose Motive Power Crane is in tow. The locomotive, the chalked inscription on the cab-side symptomatic of its neglected appearance, carries a BR class 4 plain blastpipe and a small stove-pipe chimney fitted in August 1955, the result of draughting and steaming trials carried out by Swindon Works, which vastly improved the steaming and reduced coal consumption. The wooded backcloth to the north of Buxted, climbing up to the Crowborough Beacon foothills, provides a morning sunshine setting to the crane movement timed for a 9 a.m. departure from Brighton to Tunbridge Wells on 7th July 1962.

J.J. Smith

164 Another of the class, No. 30534, fitted with a Lemaître blastpipe and large diameter chimney, has its generous goods train (by Central Section secondary line standards) well in hand. The 9.12 a.m. Groombridge–Lewes goods is eased through Buxted on 24th June 1961, in one of the most scenic and open photographic locations in Sussex, with the backcloth of the undulating lower slopes of the Crowborough Downs and High Hurstwood's forested slopes on the horizon.

S.C. Nash

165 Steam literally in the landscape near Burnt Oak Bridge between Crowborough and Buxted. On 5th April 1916, D Class tank locomotive No. 273 was working the 8.0 a.m. Tunbridge Wells to Brighton at just under 50 m.p.h. when it left the rails, and some seventy yards further on crashed over on to its side, turned completely round and came to rest upside down with the wheels spinning madly. All but one of the coaches came off the track, but injuries to passengers were slight. Blame was placed on the permanent way foreman for leaving the track unsuitable for passage at speed, and giving no warning. No. 273 was a distinctly accident prone engine, having crashed into a rockfall near High Rocks in 1883, and the following year figured in an incident involving taking a drunken major into the cab. In this photograph the unfortunate victim has been craned on to its side, providing a rare view down through the hole left by the missing chimney. Its recovery certainly attracted a considerable crowd, including the military, and in the background the Crowborough foothills as yet retain a distinctly wintry appearance. *H.M. Madgwick Collection*

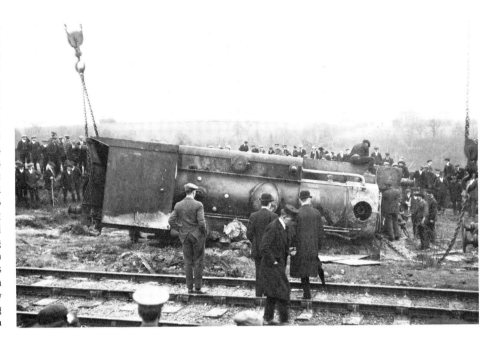

166 A northbound local working slows through the sunlit cutting for its Crowborough stop, having traversed the 1,022 yards-long tunnel after reaching the summit of the line. In addition to the 'Birdcage' set the train boasts a pre-grouping luggage van, and next to the locomotive a former LB&SCR horse box. The engine is No. 2050, a Lawson Billinton rebuild of his father's B4 class 4-4-0. Twelve B4s were converted to class B4X, the first pair in 1922, but work on the remainder continued into the year following the grouping. Performance was disappointing, comparing unfavourably with Maunsell's rebuilds of the Wainwright class Ds and Es. Following electrification of the Brighton main line the class was relegated to local secondary services in East and Central Sussex, particularly the Uckfield line, as seen here. The locomotive is in pre-war Maunsell green livery, and was probably based at Stewarts Lane at the time the picture was taken. Both classes had an intermittent post-war career, spending months on end in store, and all had gone by the end of 1951.

Lens of Sutton

167 The other side of the climb to Crowborough Tunnel is portrayed dramatically in this late summer 1951 photograph, the gradient of 1 in 75/80 for over three miles speaking for itself as E Class 4-4-0 No. 31176 lifts the 11.8 a.m. Tonbridge–Brighton service round the curve past Redgate Mill Farm, set in the glorious Wealden patchwork of open fields grafted onto the prevailing woodland. The additional coach between the locomotive and the 'Birdcage' 3-set is one of the former straight-sided second class vehicles used on Continental boat trains to Dover and Folkestone. The date is 20th August 1951, less than a fortnight before 31176's withdrawal. *S.C. Nash*

168 Prior to the doubling of the Crowborough line south of Eridge in 1894, the Lewes and Polegate lines were operated as two independent tracks. The 9.18 a.m. Tunbridge Wells–Brighton train curves out of Eridge with the double-eaved station frontage appearing behind the parapets of the road bridge. D1 Class No. 31505 has steam to spare on the sunny morning of 14th April 1952. This class of Maunsell rebuilds spent nearly all their working days on the Eastern Section, but those based at Bricklayers Arms, as was No. 31505 briefly at this time, had diagrams which took them on to the Central Section. *J.J. Smith*

169 Eridge Station is in the middle of nowhere, as rural a junction station as could be found. Today its junction aura is over, following the Tunbridge Wells–Eridge closure in 1985. Late spring is just turning into summer deep in the Wealden heartland, the oasthouse of Forge Farm on the right very much a Kentish feature having spilled over into this part of Sussex. At this point the county border is less than two miles distant. An up empty coaching stock working timetabled as the 8.36 a.m. Tunbridge Wells–Eridge has just passed Birchden Junction, whose signal box and up junction signals are visible in the distance, to make the last couple of hundred yards into Eridge Station behind BR Standard Class 4 No. 80144. This class dominated the final years of the Central Section's local steam-hauled services. *T. Stephens*

170 Groombridge Junction, in an almost arboretum-like setting, in early Southern Railway days with a delightful all-'Brighton' train taking the north side of the triangle of lines from Tunbridge Wells. The locomotive is one of the five I4 class 4-4-2Ts which were then Nos. B31 to B35. Their existence came about in an interesting fashion. Construction of ten boilers for the class I2 was shared equally between Brighton Works and the North British Locomotive Company. The latter were seven or eight months late in delivery, so Marsh decided to make up lost time by replacing the anticipated late arrivals with five of home construction using saturated steam. When the North British boilers arrived Marsh used these in 1908/9 for five new engines classified I4, though there was little difference between them and the five superheated I2s. By 1927 all the I4s were concentrated at Tunbridge Wells. They performed disappointingly compared to the closely related I3s. Withdrawal commenced in January 1936 with No. 2031, and concluded with the breaking-up of No. 2034 at Eastleigh in May 1940. *Lens of Sutton*

171 A fine ground level picture, again at Groombridge Junction, but keen observers will have noted the repositioning of the junction signal to the up side. In a powerful portrait E4 Class No. 32582 swings a Tunbridge Wells West to Oxted working on to the spur line to Ashurst Junction on 3rd October 1953. The Maunsell coaches bear the 'plum and spilt milk' livery.

S.C. Creer

172 Groombridge Junction yet again, but with no apology. Quite apart from the snowy setting emphasising the contrast between light and dark, the picture is full of new interest. The turn of the year reveals a preponderance of evergreen trees, while behind the bare silver birches the outline of a chapel without tower or spire is discerned. It was doubtless built at a time when it was LB&SCR practice not to run trains during church hours. The train too is unusual, an L1 Class 4-4-0 hauling *ex*-LB&SCR push-pull set No. 715. After a lifetime of service on the Eastern Section, the whole class was transferred to store at Nine Elms following the Kent Coast lines electrification. A few were brought out for Christmas parcels traffic, but two were briefly transferred to Tonbridge, including No. 31756, during which spell it is seen working the 2.0 p.m. Tunbridge Wells West–Oxted service on 16th January 1960.

L.W. Rowe

173 Groombridge Station, close to the Kentish border, comprised staggered platforms linked by a subway, and was traditionally well-kept with very neat areas of lawn and flowerbeds seen in the foreground. Lines into Groombridge opened as follows: from East Grinstead and Tunbridge Wells West 1st October 1866, from Uckfield 3rd August 1868, the 'Cuckoo' line from Hailsham 1st September 1880, and the cut-off line from Oxted 1st October 1888. A fine LB&SCR goods shed contrasts with the roof of the modern signal box just visible behind the canopy of the island platform, from which BR Standard tank locomotive No. 80017 is departing in charge of the 1.45 p.m. Tunbridge Wells West–Eastbourne train on 24th March 1962.

L.W. Rowe

174 The High Rocks, a picturesque outcrop of the tough central Wealden sandstone which the erosion of softer strata has left isolated atop a woodland ridge of Broadwater Forest, was exactly the kind of natural wonder that would entice Edwardian holidaymakers. The possibilities of pleasure traffic were not lost upon the LB&SCR directors, who opened a halt there on 1st June 1907. On view is the platform for Tunbridge Wells, the one serving the Groombridge direction being on the other side of the road bridge from which the photograph was taken, separate sets of stairs descending to each platform. The opening coincided with the introduction of rail motor services from Tunbridge Wells West, but ordinary traffic was negligible with no village close by and only a hostelry by the roadside to quench the thirst of returning hikers. The halt was an early casualty of hostilities in 1939, reopening under wartime circumstances in 1942, but finally closed ten years later. This picture was taken when High Rocks Halt was still open, with indications of decay very evident on the corrugated iron shelter and enamel signs. Q Class No. 30546 of Horsham shed slows for the stop, as passengers intent on disembarking stand at the doorways.

Lens of Sutton

THE CUCKOO LINE

175 The 4.35 p.m. Tunbridge Wells West to Eastbourne, carrying a through portion from Victoria at the rear, coasts down the easy grades approaching Polegate from the north on 7th September 1950. The locomotive is Marsh J2 Class 4-6-2T No. 32326 which, when built in 1912, bore the name of *Bessborough*. At the close of the same month, with the new LMS-designed 2-6-4 tank locomotives infiltrating the area, this former LB&SCR show-piece was transferred to Brighton and scrapped the following summer. Here it still carries its post-war green livery and, as yet, no BR smokebox numberplate, retaining its number on the buffer beam. It is travelling on the original line opened from Polegate to Hailsham in 1849. When the line north to Eridge was opened in 1880, the Hailsham line was diverted at Polegate to allow through running to Eastbourne instead of Lewes.   *J.J. Smith*

176 The scenery south of Hailsham provides a pleasant setting in the bright morning light of 26th June 1951 of a rarely photographed working, at least on the lower end of the line. C2X No. 32543, just transferred to Eastbourne but still carrying a 75A (Brighton) shedplate, takes the 7.10 a.m. Polegate to Tunbridge Wells West goods up the line. The guard's brake van is passing Malbrooks Crossing down distant signal. The southern section to Hailsham skirted the western side of Pevensey Level, with shallow cuttings where it traversed spurs of higher ground near Polegate, Summer Hill (which the train is approaching) and at Hailsham.

J.J. Smith

177 A pairing of pre-grouping rolling stock that made it through to nationalisation! Veteran D Class 4-4-0 No. 31731, somewhat run-down yet still graceful, eases a pair of LB&SCR coaches away from Hailsham, whose outskirts can be seen in the distance. The actual location is Leap Cross, the faint afternoon sunshine just reflecting off the 4.39 p.m. Eastbourne to Tunbridge Wells West train. The 'Cuckoo' section northwards, opened through to Eridge on 1st September 1880, was part of a deal with the South Eastern Railway allowing the latter a share of the Eastbourne receipts in return for the LB&SCR consolidating its flank in East Sussex. The date is 28th March 1951, just three months before this Wainwright stalwart was retired. Incidentally, note that the weight of the locomotive exceeded that of the train. *J.J. Smith*

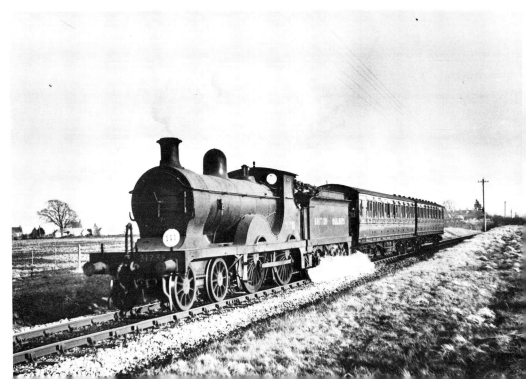

178 Any comment on Horam Station must refer to the five sets of names used during its lifetime, the one on the station nameboard being the most apt as Waldron was some two and a half miles away. Further south at Hellingly the line has followed the Cuckmere River northwards and then one of its tributaries, the Waldron Gill. The countryside has become more forested and the station here is very much in a woodland setting, with Standard Class 4MT 2-6-4T No. 80042 pausing with an up train on 9th June 1962. *D.W. Winkworth*

179 Horam Station lay in a valley, but the line climbed from the floor on a sharp 1 in 50 gradient. 'Battle of Britain' Class Pacific No. 34055 *Fighter Pilot* had seen sharper grades such as Mortehoe's 1 in 36 bank in the West Country, but is nevertheless taking things slowly under the engineman's watchful eye in hauling a far from heavy 9.5 a.m. special of thirteen wagons and a brake van from Polegate to Heathfield on 2nd July 1960. The special load carried was in fact fertiliser and, after leaving this at Heathfield, the locomotive returned to Eastbourne. This was possibly the only time a Bulleid Pacific worked a goods train over the 'Cuckoo' line. *J.J. Smith*

180 No. 34055 *Fighter Pilot* is seen returning 'light engine' through Horam Station *en route* back to Eastbourne after working the train pictured in the previous photograph. At one time profitable milk traffic was despatched through an Express Dairy plant at Horam which was served by the siding visible in the bottom right hand corner. Goods facilities were withdrawn some time prior to the line's closure; the yard, however, continued to be used by the local coal merchant for storage. Following its arrival back at Eastbourne No. 34055 was pressed into service on the 1.31 p.m. holiday train to Westhoughton, Lancashire. *J.J. Smith*

181　A South Eastern takeover in the shape of H Class 0-4-4T No. 31310 of Redhill shed and 'Birdcage' 3-set No. 571 climbing at 1 in 50 to Heathfield in the late afternoon spring sunshine. The 5.56 p.m. Eastbourne–Tunbridge Wells West is seen at Maynard's Green, just over half a mile north of Horam, on 24th April 1951. Unlike the Uckfield line, the 'Cuckoo' line was never doubled. Heathfield stands at an altitude of some 500 feet on a Wealden ridge, rich in iron ore deposits, running from east of Uckfield to Mountfield and Battle.
J.J. Smith

182 Surviving I1X Class No. 2002 curves out of Heathfield's 266 yards-long tunnel with 3-set No. 508 comprising the 4.39 p.m. Eastbourne to Tunbridge Wells West train on 12th May 1951. The tunnel was built for double track and at one time contained a headshunt which ended just beyond the northern portal visible in this picture. It was lifted at the end of World War II. The train is about to breast the summit of a virtually continuous climb for six miles from Hellingly. Heathfield was a station of character with many interesting features, notably the use of natural gas for its station lighting, distributed from a small gas works. Until 1930 a small gas engine was operated for pumping water from a 370ft borehole up into the water tower there.

J.J. Smith

183   The 'Cuckoo' line was by far the most scenic of all the LB&SCR's branch lines, traversing the heart of the Weald with its luscious foliage and undulating landscape. Climbing to Heathfield Tunnel on 16th June 1962 is the 11.10 a.m. Tonbridge to Eastbourne, formed of four Maunsell coaches and a BR Standard 3-set, a tidy load on the switchback grades even for a powerful Standard class 4MT tank locomotive, in the shape of No. 80149. The location is just south of Orchard House, which stands adjacent to the track round the bend the train has just negotiated.
S.C. Nash

184   In the heart of the Weald, climbing the 1 in 50 to Heathfield from the valley of the upper Rother, is an unusual working in the shape of the 4.30 p.m. weedkilling train from Oxted to Polegate on 3rd June 1962. Double-heading are Standard Class 4MT No. 80154, the last of the class (and final locomotive to be constructed at Brighton Works) and that which hauled the last train over the East Grinstead to Lewes (Bluebell) line in March 1958, and K Class No. 32349. The train had previously sprayed the Three Bridges to Tunbridge Wells section, where the tanks were probably replenished. Then No. 32349 propelled to Oxted and next proceeded forward to Eridge where No. 80154 was attached. Photography in this area is particularly difficult due to it being the most afforested part of the line.   *J.J. Smith*

185 Just two months prior to withdrawal, still in Southern Railway livery, I1X Class No. 2002 is seen again, this time heading southwards in the evening sunlight on 11th May 1951 with the 5.55 p.m. Tunbridge Wells West–Eastbourne. It has just crossed the stream of the Rother, barely two miles from its source just south of Rotherfield. The river lies in the valley seen at the left edge of the picture, and the train has begun the formidable two and a quarter miles climb at 1 in 50 towards Heathfield. On the opposite far side of the valley lies Mayfield.

J.J. Smith

186 Between Mayfield and Rotherfield stations lies the summit of the line, with ruling gradients of 1 in 50 to the north and 1 in 52 to the south, together with tight curves of up to 24-chains radius. Heading south out of Argos Hill Tunnel, which took the railway under the A267 main road, is a Wainwright D class, still striding along with a degree of dignity in spite of its fading livery telling that the end is uncomfortably near, in fact exactly a year away. No. 31490 of Bricklayers Arms shed gently breasts the line's summit with the 1.55 p.m. Tunbridge Wells West to Eastbourne on 22nd August 1950, as a friendly footplate crew greet the photographer.

J.J. Smith

187 Crowborough and Jarvis Brook Station, on the Uckfield line, was originally called Rotherfield until the name was transferred in August 1880 to the new station on the 'Cuckoo' line, as the village of Rotherfield was much closer. With typical LB&SCR siting to draw in the custom from the two villages of Rotherfield and of Mark Cross, both one and a half miles from the new station, its out-reach, as usual, fell between two stools. Seen here is the surviving signal box of a pair, the North box having closed in 1935. No. 80144 awaits the guard's flag, the signalman having just handed over the single line token to enable the 9.56 a.m. Tonbridge–Eastbourne train to continue its southbound course on 25th January 1964, a year and a half before the line closed – apart from the Hailsham–Polegate section which lingered on until 1968.
E. Wilmshurst

188 Approaching Rotherfield from the north on 9th February 1952 is Wainwright C Class 0-6-0 No. 31717 of Tonbridge shed with the 1.50 p.m. Tunbridge Wells West to Eastbourne, the 'Birdcage' set making it a complete SE&CR train. It has just climbed the best part of two miles from Redgate Mill Junction at a stiff 1 in 50, clearly defined when comparing the levelled headshunt of the siding with the rising line coming past the left-hand side of the signal.
J.J. Smith

189 Bopeep Junction, named after an inn on what is now the outskirts of St. Leonards, and frequented by shepherds from the nearby marsh pastures, is the southern point of the South Eastern Railway's 1852 route from London to Hastings. This runs across the hilly Weald for twenty-seven miles from Tunbridge Wells. The stretch into Hastings presented many problems due to the varied strata and underground springs, and a single line only was in use until 1906 because of restricted clearances. The 2.10 p.m. Hastings to Charing Cross train headed by 'Schools' Class No. 30910 *Merchant Taylors* is seen emerging from Bopeep Tunnel on 7th June 1958, the final day of steam-hauled services. West St. Leonards Station's platforms were in the process of being lengthened to accommodate up to two sets of the new narrow-bodied 6-car diesel units built for this line. *L.W. Rowe*

THE HASTINGS LINE

190 The 6.57 p.m. West St. Leonards to Crowhurst has ex-LB&SCR D3 Class 0-4-4T No. 32388 sandwiched between a pair of push-pull sets, 660 leading and 661 trailing, these services necessitated by the prolonged closure of Bopeep Tunnel for repairs. The date is 4th June 1950 at a period when main line trains ran instead to Bexhill West. The location is just north of West St. Leonards where the line is on a gentle curve, and also a gradient of 1 in 100. This was always a favourite spot for photographers. *J.J. Smith*

191 The 6.35 p.m. Hastings to Sevenoaks comprising SE&CR-designed 6-set No. 636 is in the charge of L Class 4-4-0 No. 31766 of Tonbridge shed. Although taken on 31st July 1955, the scene is a play-back to the immediate post-grouping years when this class and rolling stock reigned supreme over this line, before Maunsell and the 'Schools' class diluted the old South Eastern image.   *J.J. Smith*

192 The Hastings line will always be associated with Richard Maunsell's 'Schools' class locomotives, the most powerful 4-4-0s built in this country, and they proved ideally competent to cope with the sharp gradients and winding curves on this route. By careful design their dimensions just fell within the loading gauge of the several narrow tunnels on the line. No. 30902 *Wellington* seems perfectly at ease with the 2.10 p.m. Hastings to Charing Cross train on 24th August 1957, comprising seven Maunsell coaches with a 3-set at either end of the formation. The train is leaving behind the outskirts of St. Leonards as it climbs towards Crowhurst.   *D.T. Rowe*

193 The curve here is the sharp one seen just behind the end of the train in the previous photograph. In the much more treeless landscape of the late Edwardian period, Wainwright D Class 4-4-0 No. 741 gingerly eases past some embankment repairs as it descends the Battle Ridge into Hastings with the 3.45 p.m. Pullman from Cannon Street. It has been suggested that lineside instability was caused by the use of the sand and clay that had caused so much trouble in the Bopeep Tunnel construction. The permanent way gang appear well-organised with the foreman watchful of security, and with a planked walkway for wheelbarrows and a makeshift shelter.   *Lens of Sutton*

194 Steam in harmony with the landscape, but a view both attractive and interesting since across the valley lies the seventeen-arch 417 yards-long Filsham, or Sidley, Viaduct carrying away south-west the branch to Bexhill West. The lines meet at Crowhurst. The express in the picture, complete with Pullman Car, is the 1.2 p.m. Cannon Street to Hastings on 24th August 1957, hauled by 'Schools' 4-4-0 No. 30926 *Repton*, which was recently brought back from preservation in the U.S.A. and restored to working order on the North Yorkshire Moors Railway. *D.T. Rowe*

195 The County of Kent is more associated with hop-fields than Sussex, but even so, a few spilled over the border into East Sussex. When the hops ripened in late summer, special trains were provided for the hop-pickers, who were usually poor families from the East End of London taking a week's paid 'holiday' away from the grime of the metropolis. When the end of the holiday week came round, the special hop-pickers' trains had to be worked up from St. Leonards depot to Bodiam on the Kent and East Sussex line. The 4.40 p.m. up empty stock working on 8th September 1957 is on its way, first to Robertsbridge where one of the 'Terriers' will run round to attach itself to the rear of the train, as such a movement was not possible at Bodiam. The leading 'Terrier' is No. 32670, originally K&ESR No. 3, which was purchased by the Rother Valley Railway from the LB&SCR in 1901, and today as No. 3 *Bodiam* is back on its former stamping ground. Its grimy companion, No. 32678, carries a chalked inscription on its cabside referring to the '6.5 Special'. This probably refers to a popular BBC Television programme of Rock 'n' Roll music which went out at five past six every Saturday night. Its initial opening sequence had a railway theme, and the programme starred Don Lang and his Frantic Five. The location of the photograph is by the woodland just south of Crowhurst. *J.J. Smith*

196 Approaching Sidley after crossing the viaduct is Bulleid Q1 Class 0-6-0 No. 33036 of Tonbridge shed with the 5.52 p.m. Tonbridge to Bexhill West train on 21st May 1956. The formation consists of Maunsell 3-coach corridor sets Nos. 948 and 940 and two *ex*-SE&CR third class coaches Nos. 1106 and 1082. The viaduct was constructed between 1898 and 1900, and required over nine million bricks and the moving of over 300,000 cubic yards of spoil. Its 70ft-high arches were blown apart when it was spectacularly demolished on 23rd May 1969, the branch having closed to all traffic from 15th June 1964. *J.J. Smith*

197 The Crowhurst, Sidley and Bexhill Railway, with heavy SER backing, was a bid to capture a slice of the traffic generated by the holiday resorts lying west of Hastings, until then the monopoly of the LB&SCR. The construction of the branch, which was just over four miles long and opened in 1902, necessitated the provision of a spacious junction station with bay platforms at Crowhurst. Gradients of 1 in 90 and 1 in 170 were required on either side of the dip down to the viaduct. Bexhill West Station was also grandiose with an engine shed off the picture on the right. The 'A' signal box north of the station was palatial, while the 'B' cabin is seen at the end of the middle road enhancing the station building behind. Its levers operated the crossover. H Class 0-4-4T No. 31162 of St. Leonards shed stands at the remaining covered platform with its push-pull set on 19th April 1958. *D.W. Winkworth*

198 On 18th October 1959, a ten-coach enthusiasts' special ran from Victoria double-headed by L Class Nos. 31760 and 31768 to Robertsbridge. The main portion of the train was worked to Tenterden by Lancing Works' A1 Class 'Terrier' No. DS680 (formerly LB&SCR *Waddon*, SE&CR No. 751 and today preserved in Canada) and at the other end A1X Class No. 32670 (former K&ESR No. 3 *Bodiam*, and since restored to its former status). Here four coaches are seen being re-attached to the six coaches of the main train after its arrival back at Robertsbridge from Tenterden. The latter formation included green-liveried Pullman Car No. 182. Typical of the era of branch line railtours, quite a number of interested spectators have assumed the freedom of the tracks. The moderate heights of part of Sealands Wood on the horizon, though already crowned with housing, still give the outskirts of Robertsbridge a very rural atmosphere.   *D.H. Ballantyne*

199 An eastbound 'Terrier' is seen with a ballast special near Junction Road on 28th September 1952 in the valley of the River Rother, which has its rise some ten miles away near Mayfield. The Rother Valley Railway opened in 1900. There was a private platform provided for access to the adjoining fields by shooting parties, and in 1903 Colonel Stephens applied for permission to open the platform to the public. According to its nameboard it was 'Junction Road for Hawkhurst', the latter town some four miles away, and the platform was built of wood and earth. In 1947/8 the wooden facing was replaced with concrete slabs. It boasted a short siding laid in 1909 on the Robertsbridge side of the A229 which was shunted by resorting to tow roping, a practice which continued into the 1950s.   *J.J. Smith*

200 Near Junction Road again, but this time the scenic approach from the east is seen with the halt just out of the picture on the right. The River Rother flows away eastwards across the foreground, having passed under the railway a few hundred yards to the west, and yet again by Hodson's flour mill further upstream outside Robertsbridge. The strange terrace of vat-like buildings in the background are in fact oast houses of a less common square design used for drying hops. Threading its way past the tall trees, tinged with the first touch of spring, is the 3.30 p.m. special from Tenterden Town to Robertsbridge with 'Terrier' No. 3 *Bodiam*, with steam to spare, having just one coach and a gentle downhill run. The date is 11th April 1966, five years after the formation of the Kent and East Sussex Railway Preservation Society to resuscitate the line. *Bodiam* was delivered to Robertsbridge on 11th April 1964, stored in the open in the goods yard, and in the following months employed on shunting duties at Hodson's mill. It ran a few special workings along the line, but in 1967 Mrs. Barbara Castle, then Minister of Transport, refused to grant an order for reopening because of disruptions which would allegedly have been caused by the level crossings over the busy A21 and A229 roads. The through connection westwards from Bodiam had to be foregone before the preservation society reached an agreement.

S.C. Nash

201 Another of the early special workings, a stock train from Robertsbridge to Rolvenden, nears Bodiam on 30th May 1966. The train includes two Pullman cars built in 1927 for the Hastings line. They conform to the rigorous Restriction '0' loading gauge to enable them to work through the cramped tunnels on the Hastings line. They were acquired at the eleventh hour from a scrap dealer in Cardiff. This picturesque setting between Robertsbridge and Bodiam with field upon field of poles supporting the burgeoning hops, is typical of the Sussex/Kent border, but a reduction in consumption and an increasing accent on lager has seen a dramatic shrinkage in the hop industry, and especially in acreage. Soon settings like this could be a thing of the past. Former LB&SCR 'Terrier' 0-6-0T locomotive No. 32650 provided the motive power along a section of track since abandoned.

J.G. Mallinson

202 Approaching Wadhurst, whose station lies in an arc of wooded cuttings, the 4.50 p.m. Hastings to Charing Cross train has just left the 1,025 yards-long Wadhurst Tunnel hauled by 'Schools' Class No. 30935 *Sevenoaks*, of Bricklayers Arms shed, on 25th May 1957. The photographer, who wrote a book about the class, described these capable and elegant locomotives as 'the best 4-4-0s that ever ran'. The first pair of coaches are of SE&CR origin, followed by Restriction '0' coaches. The scenery is typical of the High Weald; the border with Kent is just three miles away, and a further three beyond ran the Hawkhurst branch on an almost parallel route.   *D.W. Winkworth*

203 In spite of an attempt by the Brighton, Lewes & Hastings Company which succeeded in obtaining powers to extend its line through to Ashford, Parliament had second thoughts, being persuaded that the South Eastern could better operate this section. This was opened in 1851, notwithstanding a second battle of Hastings in February of that year in which the rival companies resorted to holding up each other's trains – standing a ballast train at the neck of the carriage sidings, tearing up the track, erecting a barrier across the station approach, and marooning the LB&SCR agent in his office! 'Schools' Class No. 30931 *King's Canterbury* with the 11.39 a.m. Hastings–Ashford is seen getting to grips with the considerable climb to Ore on a stretch of 1 in 60 (note the catch points) between Mount Pleasant Tunnel and the much longer 1,402 yards-long Ore Tunnel on 24th May 1958. The sandstone hills comprising a jigsaw of strata, termed the Hastings Beds, are well developed with housing, a large part laid out in terraces.
L.W. Rowe

HASTINGS TO ASHFORD

204 When the railway first arrived at Rye in 1851, the River Tillingham was crossed on a swing bridge. As a result of a short branch being provided round to Rye Harbour in 1854, river traffic through this point so declined that a replacement fixed bridge was substituted in 1903, and the Southern Railway later installed a tied girder bridge with delightfully styled abutment facings. By the time of this photograph, the windmill had undergone several alterations and a facelift, being used in turn as a pottery and a dwelling. L1 Class No. 31759 takes the 11.55 a.m. Ashford–Hastings across the river on 7th May 1955, the clean looking 'Birdcage' set an ideal match. The Brede, Tillingham and Rother rivers all merge at Rye, east of which commence the levels of the Romney Marsh which the line to Ashford follows for a large part of its length across the border into Kent, just two miles away. Malaria died out there only two generations ago, and the rich pastures support many thousands of sheep, the result of drainage schemes reclaiming much arable farmland for a whole range of new crops, including asparagus.
LCGB Ken Nunn Collection

205 In Southern Railway days locomotives of the rival pre-grouping companies were now free to work in each other's preserves, and it is particularly noteworthy to find a Stroudley 'Gladstone', No. B174, working eastwards to Ashford. As the class began to be pared down in the mid-1920s, the survivors gravitated to Brighton shed, a regular 'Gladstone' class duty being the 9.10 a.m. Brighton–Ashford – in all probability the train photographed here – and the 1.20 p.m. return working from Ashford. No. B174 was withdrawn in 1929. The setting is the bridge across the River Tillingham at Rye with the famous windmill, a landmark for miles in this flat south-eastern corner of Sussex.   *Lens of Sutton*

Steam still survives in the Sussex landscape at the Bluebell Railway which has preserved the five miles long section of line from Sheffield Park to Horsted Keynes. E4 Class 0-6-2T No. 473, *Birch Grove*, was photographed at the latter location in the early 1970s.

J.S. Everitt

ACKNOWLEDGEMENTS

The authors gratefully acknowledge the assistance generously provided by a large number of people, without whose help this album would never have seen the light of day. In particular we wish to thank Stephen Mourton, of Runpast Publishing, who gave us complete freedom regarding the selection of illustrations and layout, and also Chris Evans, who carefully edited the captions and provided much helpful criticism. The proofs were kindly checked by Chris Evans and David J. Fakes. We would like to offer a sincere *thank you* to the following, who assisted in the compilation of this volume: Hugh Ballantyne, J.R. Besley, Chris Campbell, Derek Clayton, Lewis Coles, Stanley Creer, David Cross, Hugh Davies, John Dewing, John Everitt, Ted Gamblin, Peter Groom, Bill Jackson, H.N. James, J.H.W. Kent, R.W. Kidner, Rodney Lissenden, Phil Lynch, Graham Mallinson, Tony Molyneaux, Brian Morrison, Gavin Morrison, Sid Nash, Ken Nichols, John Price, D. Trevor Rowe, Lyndon Rowe, John Scrace, Gerald Siviour, John J. Smith, John Smith (of Lens of Sutton), Graham Stacey, Tim Stephens, David Wallis, Edwin Wilmshurst, John P. Wilson, Peter Winding, Derek Winkworth, also the staff of the Library at the National Railway Museum, York, and Worthing Reference Library.

BIBLIOGRAPHY

Geoffrey Body – *Railways of the Southern Region* – Patrick Stephens
Donald Bradley – *Locomotives of the LB&SCR* Vols. 1–3 – RCTS
Edwin Course – *The Railways of Southern England – Secondary and Branch Lines* – Batsford
C. Hamilton Ellis – *The London Brighton and South Coast Railway* – Ian Allan
J.T. Howard Turner – *The London Brighton & South Coast Railway* Vols. 1–3 – Batsford
C. Dendy Marshall – *A History of the Southern Railway* – Ian Allan
Vic Mitchell and Keith Smith – *Branch Lines, Southern Main Lines and South Coast Railways* series – Middleton Press.
H.P. White – *A Regional History of the Railways of Great Britain Vol. 2 Southern England* – Phoenix